MORE LONDON'S
STRANGEST TALES

MORE LONDON'S
STRANGEST TALES

TOM QUINN

First published in Great Britain in 2015 by
The Robson Press (an imprint of Biteback Publishing Ltd)
Westminster Tower
3 Albert Embankment
London SE1 7SP
Copyright © Tom Quinn 2015

ISBN 978-1-84954-918-9

10 9 8 7 6 5 4 3 2 1

A CIP catalogue record for this book is available from the British Library.

Set in Adobe Caslon Pro

Printed and bound in Great Britain by
CPI Group (UK) Ltd, Croydon CR0 4YY

INTRODUCTION

The success of the original *London's Strangest Tales*, which was published almost ten years ago, prompted me to wander ever further along the byways of London's history to discover more remarkable, odd, quirky and sometimes bizarre stories. This book contains the very best of these, and represents years of research and trawling through obscure, long-forgotten newspapers and books.

London has such a fascinating and complex history that it is hardly surprising there are so many stories still to be told, but even I was amazed at the masses of wonderful material I was able to unearth second time around, as it were.

Here, you will find stories of ghosts and eccentrics, mad vicars and dotty aristocrats, all of whom left their mark on what might best be called the alternative history of England's capital.

In addition to these stories, there are strange tales about the structural environment and the physical landscape of London; its parks and rivers, graveyards and houses, churches and offices.

Of course, as buildings have been altered, refurbished or demolished over the centuries, the whole landscape of the capital has changed, but Londoners are inherently conservative and, often for no apparent reason (other than, perhaps, for sentimentality's sake), they like to ensure that parts of ancient and significant buildings are left hidden in odd corners long after the original buildings have changed use or been pulled down. In other cases, sections of old buildings are incorporated into new buildings or preserved in basements or attics. If you want to find these strange and surprising survivors, this is the book for you.

Much of *More London's Strangest Tales* concerns itself with the old City, the famous square mile, but there are also stories from the distant suburbs and from south of the river – 'London over the water', as it has long been known.

Perhaps best of all, *More London's Strangest Tales* gives you both an unusual history of one of the world's great cities, as well as a guide to some of its least-known and most unusual surviving treasures.

Happy exploring!

TWEAKING
NAPOLEON'S NOSE

∽⊶⊷∽

The large semi-circular building at the Trafalgar Square entrance to the Mall has a curious history. It was commissioned by King Edward VII in memory of his mother Queen Victoria and completed in 1912. The architect was Sir Aston Webb who also refronted Buckingham Palace just down the road.

Successive governments have been allowed the use of a flat in Admiralty Arch but it is mostly used now as offices. It also has a curious feature that has never been fully explained.

There are four arches through the building: two for pedestrians and two central arches for road traffic. On the wall of the northern traffic arch, some six feet off the ground, a life-size brass nose sticks out of the stonework.

The nose is at just the right height to be clearly visible to anyone passing who happens to be riding a horse and, given that horse transport still dominated London when the building was completed, it seems almost certain that the nose was one of Edward VII's little jokes.

He was notoriously fond of gags and some believe he had the nose designed in the shape of Napoleon's so that passing cavalry officers (and anyone else on horseback) could give it a good tweak or a punch as they passed by.

The other theory is that, as Edward actually hated Victoria, who died in 1901, he had the nose designed to look like his mother's so he could get his revenge on her each time he passed by it.

TAXING TIMES

The British government has a reputation going back centuries for trying to find ingenious new ways to tax the public. The trick today is to find a tax that it is difficult to avoid. Of course taxes – as someone famously once said – are for little people, and wealthy members of government have themselves always been as keen as any private citizen millionaire to find ways to avoid tax.

In previous centuries, wool was taxed along with salt. At various times there have been attempts to tax wallpaper, fireplaces and even bricks. Taxing things people simply can't do without was and is also popular – which is why alcohol has always been so heavily taxed. It also explains why smuggling became such a huge industry on the south coast of England in the seventeenth and eighteenth centuries.

Recent tax dodges by large firms and wealthy individuals who simply moved their cash overseas (while claiming to be good citizens) were perhaps inevitable.

But taxing land and property rather than other forms of wealth was always a better idea because it's not so easy to move your land and your house out of the country.

However, tax avoidance was not the reason for the introduction of a window tax in England in 1696. As the title of the act makes clear, the new tax was to grant 'to His Majesty several Rates or Duties upon

Houses for making good the Deficiency of the clipped Money'.

'Clipped money' refers to the habit of ordinary citizens biting small pieces off the edges of valuable coins – which made sense when coins were still actually made of gold and silver.

At this time, income tax did not exist – in fact, income tax in the form in which we know it today did not exist until as recently as the mid-1840s.

The window tax was simply based on how many windows you had. There were exemptions for the poor and for those rooms deemed to be dairies or pantries, however, which caused a sudden increase in the number of rooms labelled 'dairy' or 'cheese room'. Until the modern habit of completely rebuilding house interiors began in the 1980s and 1990s, it was still possible to see the old painted dairy sign above rooms in old houses.

But, despite attempts to avoid the tax in this way, those with houses with anything between ten and twenty windows were charged a flat rate of four shillings (about £25 in today's money); if your house had more than twenty windows you had to pay eight shillings (£50).

For houses with fewer than nine windows, a flat rate of two shillings was charged, but of course no sooner was the tax introduced than people began to try to avoid it, which is why we still see many early eighteenth-century houses with many of their windows bricked up.

The tax lasted until 1850, when a particularly dark and gloomy winter made people feel that the window tax was really a tax on light and air. It was finally repealed in 1851, but of course no one wanted to pay the cost of removing the bricks from those long-bricked-up windows, which is why they have lasted to this day.

JIMMY'S BONES

When the church of St James Garlickhythe was rebuilt by Christopher Wren after the Great Fire of London, the front door opened on to the approach to Old London Bridge. In fact, you were almost on the bridge itself as you left the church.

When Old London Bridge was demolished, the new bridge was built a short distance upstream and now the church door opens on to a small area surrounded on three sides by ugly modern buildings and on the other side by a four-lane highway.

Inside, by contrast, the church has altered little in more than three centuries and until the 1950s one of the church's more bizarre relics was the mummified corpse of Jimmy Garlickhythe standing upright in a glass box.

Jimmy's skin was extraordinarily well preserved and his thick hair was still visible on his head. His features were made ghoulish by the addition of two fake but brightly painted wooden eyes.

It is still possible – if you ask the vicar nicely – to see Jimmy, but he is kept out of the public eye these days in a cupboard. The assumption is that today's visitors are rather more squeamish than their ancestors.

AMONG THE DEAD

❧⸻❦⸻☙

Few London theatre-goers realise that an evening in the theatre is often an evening among the dead.

The Theatre Royal has a number of ghosts, but the strangest is 'the Man in Grey' who has been seen regularly for more than a century. While most spirits and ghoulish apparitions tend to come out at night, the Man in Grey appears during daylight hours – more specifically, between 10 a.m. and 4 p.m.

He haunts the oldest theatre in London while clothed in a long grey cloak and an old-fashioned three-cornered hat of the type often worn by eighteenth-century gentlemen. On one occasion, more than 150 people in a matinee audience saw him simultaneously, although another hundred watching the same performance said they saw nothing at all. Some actors have said they've felt a pat on the back during a show and Harry Secombe insisted he saw the ghost in his dressing room in the summer of 1960.

The appearance of the ghost may be linked to a gruesome discovery more than a century and a half ago.

In 1850, during rebuilding work at the theatre, the skeleton of a man with a dagger still embedded in his ribs was found in a previously unknown and long bricked-up room. It is within feet of this site that the Man in Grey most often makes his presence known, but nobody knows who he is.

CHEPE HOUSES

London's Cheapside was once one of Europe's most remarkable streets. A long row of fine houses that overlooked an ancient market ('chepe' is the Saxon word for a market) was destroyed first by the Great Fire of London and then in the twentieth century it was destroyed once again by German bombers and post-war developers. Today most of the street is hideous.

But a curious tale links one of the few early buildings that remain in Cheapside and are built on a human scale.

On the corner of Wood Street and Cheapside there are two small, apparently mid-Victorian buildings that hide much earlier structures. One contains a beautiful seventeenth-century staircase supposedly designed by Sir Christopher Wren. The terms of the centuries-old lease on the buildings apparently forbids in perpetuity the building of anything higher than the existing buildings. For once the lawyers were on the side of protecting historic buildings – even *they* realised it would be very difficult to twist the terms of the lease to allow yet another monstrous carbuncle to be built on the site.

An even more remarkable survivor is the enormous London plane tree that rises behind the little buildings. The tree marks the site of the old church of St Peter in Chepe, which was destroyed in the Great

Fire. Modern, faceless office blocks loom over the part of the churchyard that remains and from which the tree grows.

This delightful corner has long intrigued artists. In the collection of poems that was to make William Wordsworth and his friend Samuel Taylor Coleridge famous – *Lyrical Ballads* of 1798 – there is a poem called 'The Reverie of Poor Susan'. Here the corner of Wood Street and Chepeside is recalled:

At the corner of Wood Street, when day-light appears,
Hangs a Thrush that sings loud, it has sung for three years:
   Poor Susan has passed by the spot, and has heard
   In the silence of morning the song of the bird.

   'Tis a note of enchantment; what ails her? She sees
     A mountain ascending, a vision of trees;
   Bright volumes of vapour through Lothbury glide,
   And a river flows on through the vale of Cheapside.

THE BONE COLLECTION

When the Victorian Spitalfields Market just east of the City was being redeveloped in the 1990s, there was a real danger that the whole area would be obliterated and turned into yet more dull, monotonous (but probably iconic) office blocks.

A compromise of sorts was reached between the profit-crazed developers and those interested in preserving as much as possible of London's historic fabric. As a result, the Victorian market buildings remain along with a mix of new buildings.

During work on Bishop's Square, a remarkable and bizarre discovery was made.

Beneath what had once been the graveyard of the long-demolished monastic foundation of St Mary Spital, from which the market gets its name, was discovered a remarkably well-preserved charnel house dating from around 1320. A charnel house is rather like a crypt but used to hold the bones of the dead. The charnel house or ossuary at Spitalfields appears to have been built thirty or forty years after the foundation of the priory itself. It was the crypt of the chapel of St Mary Magdalene and St Edmund the Bishop, part of the priory foundation.

When rediscovered in 1999, the charnel house still contained countless bones. Despite its importance, the developers would have been happy to destroy it or simply move it elsewhere, thus ending its relationship with the local area, but wiser counsels prevailed and the charnel house was left where it was found, although incorporated into the new office building. It can now be viewed by appointment via a special basement.

As work went ahead to preserve the charnel house, thousands of other burials were discovered in what had been the surrounding graveyard and later the gardens of the Georgian terraced houses.

It was traditional in graveyards to bury the dead and then gradually move across the graveyard filling the space. When the space had entirely filled up, the grave diggers would return to the oldest side of the graveyard, remove the old graves and store the bones in a charnel house. It was simply a way to reuse the space while treating the remains with respect.

St Mary Spital was one of London's biggest priories. When built it would have been on the edge of the city, with fields and scattered farms away to the east.

When the priory was closed by Henry VIII in 1539, the crypt and chapel were not destroyed but adapted for use as a house. The last buildings were demolished at the beginning of the eighteenth century and new houses rose above it. A century later, no one recalled what lay beneath the gardens of those houses.

WATERMAN'S REST

London's Bankside retains a few glimmers of its ancient past. In Elizabethan times people crossed the river for pleasure, for Bankside and Southwark were famous for their brothels, or 'stews' as they were known. Respectable people lived north of the river and kept quiet about their regular visits to the stews over the water. The religious hypocrite who condemned the pleasures of the south bank while regularly enjoying the theatre, the cock pit and the brothels is a stock character in Elizabethan and Jacobean drama.

Curiously, many puritans felt the theatre was even more pernicious than the brothel, which is why in 1599 the company for whom Shakespeare wrote many of his plays dismantled their theatre at Shoreditch on the edge of the city and, having carried it across London Bridge in a series of carts, rebuilt it close to where the modern Globe now stands.

The history of the Southwark stews and theatres is of course well known. Perhaps less well known is that much of the traffic that crossed the river was not carried by the bridge – London Bridge was then the only solid river crossing. Most people crossed by boat and the watermen, one of London's most powerful guilds, manned the boats and did the rowing. Crossing London Bridge in a cart or carriage could take as long as an hour because it was so crammed with shops and houses that the traffic had to squeeze along a pathway just six feet wide in places.

So those who wanted an evening of pleasure crossed by water. Only one physical relic of the watermen remains. It is an ancient stone seat now set into a modern building in Bear Gardens, close to the river. Legend has it that the seat is exactly where it would have been three centuries ago when watermen waiting to be asked to carry someone over the river would sit and wait.

A BARN IN TOWN

The ancient gatehouse of St James's Palace still stares north up St James's Street, as it has done since Tudor times. Soon after the palace was first built, houses gradually sprang up along the road north towards what is now Piccadilly. Miraculously, one or two houses – including Lock & Co. Hatters – survive from the late seventeenth century.

Apart from two eighteenth-century gentlemen's clubs, the other buildings that line St James's date mostly from the end of the nineteenth century, their grand forms a reflection of what was seen as the power of a great empire; but take a left turn a short way up St James's Street into Blue Ball Yard and you will see a most remarkable and bizarre survivor from the days when this area was home to the palace and its farms.

The long, low building that fills two sides of the courtyard into which the alleyway opens looks remarkably like an old farm building – and that is exactly what it is. As the main St James's Street was redeveloped over the centuries, the farm to which this barn was once attached was forgotten, but it was certainly here in the seventeenth century when it was used to stable horses. A truly extraordinary survivor.

KILN FIRED

Now one of London's smartest districts, Notting Hill Gate was once notorious for drugs and violence. As late as the 1970s it was a place avoided by the respectable, but one district a little to the north and east of Notting Hill Gate was even worse. People spoke of Notting Dale and the Piggeries with a shudder, as this was one of London's poorest districts, an area where well into the twentieth century children still suffered from rickets and infant mortality rates were shocking. Some idea of the area as it was then can be gleaned from the remarkable photographs of Roger Mayne taken in the 1950s and 1960s. In the eighteenth century, the area was dominated by a racecourse that ran around what is now St John's Hill and brick and tile manufacturing was the dominant industry.

One of the oddest survivors of that far-off time is easy to miss if you don't know where to look, but it is here, down a quiet side street, that you will suddenly encounter an early nineteenth-century bottle kiln.

More often seen in the potteries district of the West Midlands, this type of kiln, with its elegant curved base and narrow chimney, is the last reminder that here high-quality clay was once dug up by the ton and made into tiles and other items.

The grand houses of Notting Hill that now change hands for millions started life in the brick pits and kilns in this part of London. Now all that remains is this brick kiln in Walmer Road.

SAND STORM

❦

It is an extraordinary fact, but a fact nonetheless, that thousands of tons of sand are blown round the world from the Sahara Desert each year. Much of this sand ends up in America and northern Europe, including London.

When a mild sandstorm hit Kensington in the 1950s, small samples of the sand were collected by one enterprising citizen and presented to the Science Museum in Kensington. Here officials confirmed that the sand did indeed originate in North Africa.

Small meteorites have also occasionally fallen on central London and even tiny sea fish swept up in a storm have been deposited on the city's streets, but strangest of all were the dozens of small frogs discovered in central London after a particularly violent electrical storm just after the Second World War.

A barber who had stepped out of his shop on Farringdon Road for a moment was hit on the head by one frog and a lady pushing a buggy on Gray's Inn Road saw two bounce off the pram's hood.

Several other people saw frogs falling that day and the story soon reached the local paper. One religious group insisted the frogs were a sign of God's displeasure and that we could all be pretty sure that the world was about to come to an end. It didn't.

HORSE AND MOTOR

Barbon Close is named after one of London's greatest developers. Born in 1640, Nicholas Barbon was trained as a physician but became a brilliant financier and property developer who funded large areas of speculative building west of the City of London. Perhaps the oddest thing about Barbon, however, was his middle name. His father had him christened Nicholas If-Jesus-Christ-Had-Not-Died-For-Thee-Thou-Hadst-Been-Damned Barebone!

Barbon Close can be found a short distance to the east of the British Museum and near the ancient lawyers' inns, and at the corner of Barbon Close is a very odd building; an eighteenth-century house still with its eighteenth-century shop window on the ground floor and a large hand-painted sign hanging on the wall nearby.

This sign, which is still in remarkably good condition, states proudly that this is the premises of G. Bailey & Sons. Horse & Motor Contractors. The survival of the sign a century and more after horses vanished from the London streets is testament to Londoners' love of the past.

ROMAN SPRING

Where Queen Victoria Street meets the old Huggin Hill, there is a tiny green space – known as Cleary Gardens – with an old brick wall on stone foundations that seem far older.

This peaceful corner has never been built on because it is the site of a Roman bath house and the *frigidarium* and *tepidarium* and other rooms remain to be excavated under the nearby houses.

Part of the Roman wall can still be seen below the Victorian wall and the spring that once served the bath house bubbled forth until fairly recently.

LADY MARY'S STEPS

Westminster Hall, the Jewel Tower and the Banqueting House are well known to visitors to London and residents alike. The last two are the remnants of the vast old complex of buildings known as Whitehall Palace. The buildings and courtyards of the old palace stretched from present-day Westminster Hall almost to Charing Cross, and halfway along what is now Whitehall was the Holbein Gate, a tall Tudor brick tower with a clock. The gatehouse tower that still stands at St James's Palace is very similar.

A French visitor called Sorbière came to London in 1665 and noted that the Banqueting House, which still stands, was easily the greatest part of the old palace. The rest, he observed, was a hodgepodge of buildings from different periods and of different sizes which had been made contiguous by all kinds of haphazard means.

There were several courtyards and in these the public would gather to watch the king take his morning walk. Others were allowed to watch the king eat lunch. Indeed, the poor king was never allowed a moment's privacy – even when he went to the lavatory he was accompanied as, despite his many privileges, he was thought of as public property. The penalties for any attack on the sovereign were so severe – hanging, drawing and quartering for example – that it was simply assumed the public would just gaze in awe at the king and that no one would dream of attacking him – a very different situation from the one we know today where the royal family is kept as far as possible from its subjects.

Almost all of the old palace was burned down in 1698. As we have seen, the Jewel Tower and the Banqueting House survived, but unbeknown to most visitors to London, two other parts of the ancient palace still survive.

The first is known as Queen Mary's Steps.

The river wall of the Tudor part of Whitehall Palace was altered in 1691 when Sir Christopher Wren built a terrace for Queen Mary that overlooked the Thames. The terrace was a little less than 300 feet long and projected around 70 feet out into the river, which is difficult to imagine today since the river is around 100 yards narrower than it once was since the embankment was built out in the late nineteenth century.

At either end of Wren's terrace, beautifully curved steps led to the river so that the king could walk down and step into the state barge.

It was long thought the steps had been destroyed along with the rest of the palace, but when a government office was being built at the site in the mid-twentieth century, the steps were uncovered and restored.

Today the curved steps to the north can be seen along with a section of the terrace and the old river wall. Sadly the steps at the southern end did not survive. Today you must view the site from the road as it is next to the main Ministry of Defence building, but the general layout and the sense that these are ancient stones are still clear.

The other fascinating part of the old palace that survives but is rarely seen is Henry VIII's wine cellar.

The cellar was built in 1536 to house the thousands of barrels of wine delivered from France each year for the use of the king and his court. Its beautiful vaulting surrounded by the damp of ancient river deposits provided a cool destination for a commodity of enormous value at the time; but when the palace burned down and subsequent houses were built, and in their turn destroyed, the cellar was forgotten until, in 1949, when the new Ministry of Defence building was being constructed, it was rediscovered deep beneath the accumulated soil levels.

The cellar, which has much of the look of a medieval church crypt, is seventy feet long and thirty wide. It was intact when rediscovered and almost undamaged. Did the developers rejoice? Not a bit. They and the government cared little for the cellar and would have been unconcerned at its destruction but for the intervention of Queen Mary who asked that it be saved.

Had anyone else asked their request would have gone unheeded, but we were still deferential to royalty in those days and the cellar *was* saved. But it was moved, not brick by brick, but wholesale. First an excavation was made all around it. The whole room was then encased in steel and concrete and lowered six metres. It was also moved three metres to the west of its original position.

Only in Britain would the authorities make it almost impossible to see this wonderful historic relic – Ministry of Defence officials hold events in the cellar but, absurdly, no one else is allowed in!

DEATH BY
BILLIARD BALL

❦❦❦❦

Billiards was meant to be an indoor version of croquet and pell-mell (a croquet-like game from which the London street Pall Mall gets its name). The billiard table meant that miniature versions of the outdoor games could be played indoors in winter or when the weather was too foul to allow outside games.

But there was a problem. How could the minia-ture balls be made so that they had a satisfying click when struck or when they hit each other? The earliest billiard balls were probably wooden or made of clay. Indeed, in poorer parts of the world clay balls were used within living memory. But devotees of billiards quickly realised that only one material produces a really superior and satisfying billiard ball: ivory.

Other materials were tried and ox bone produced a pretty good and relatively cheap ball, but ivory was always the choice of those who could afford the best.

The Duke of Norfolk's household inventory for 1588 reveals a fine collection of ivory billiard balls that were no doubt used in his long-vanished house in St James's Square. Ivory was harder and less prone to splitting than ox bone, clay or wood, but as the popu-larity of billiards grew the supply of elephants began to dry up – only six balls could be made from a large elephant tusk and ivory quickly became prohibitively expensive even for the rich.

A prize was eventually offered for anyone who could invent a billiard ball that looked, sounded and felt like ivory but could be manufactured cheaply.

The prize of $10,000 (several million in today's money) was offered by one of the biggest suppliers of billiard balls in the world – the American company Phelan & Collender. Inventors around the world began desperately searching for an alternative to ivory that would win them the prize.

At last the American scientist and inventor John Wesley Hyatt discovered in 1869 that, by dipping a wooden ball into nitrocellulose, a ball with all the properties of ivory could be made cheaply and easily. Hyatt does not seem to have been given his prize money and the reason for that may be that the balls had one or two drawbacks.

Despite not initially being given the money, Hyatt was delighted and those to whom he showed his new invention were astounded at the ease with which he made these new balls. In fact, Hyatt is still credited as the inventor of the first industrial plastic. By the 1870s, the new material – called celluloid – was being tested for various other uses.

Celluloid's life as the new wonder material quickly came to an end when, in a public house in north London, a player using the new balls took his shot and was immediately blown across the room by a deafening explosion.

What no one had realised was that nitrocellulose is to all intents and purposes the highly unstable explosive nitro-glycerine. Billiard balls hitting each other would not always explode, but they occasionally did and with increasing frequency as the balls came to be more widely used. In America there is evidence that one billiards (or it may have been pool) player, on hearing the explosion from the balls, assumed he was being fired at by his opponent. In the heat of the moment he pulled out his own gun, fired back and killed the other man.

The days of celluloid for billiard balls were over, but the material did enable one huge revolution in entertainment to take place: celluloid was the material that allowed film makers to run thousands of stills together in such a way as to create the illusion of movement. The cinema was born.

KATHERINE'S PILLAR

It is often assumed that London was never a beautiful city such as Florence or Rome. Somehow commercial success has fooled people into believing that one of the world's great capital cities was always a place of purely functional architecture – with a few notable exceptions such as St Paul's Cathedral.

This, of course, is entirely wrong and both the City of London and the city outside the ancient jurisdiction of the square mile were once very beautiful indeed architecturally.

Anyone who has seen Crosby Hall, the stone mansion moved in the 1920s from the City to Chelsea, will realise that the City of London was once a wonderful combination of elaborate timber-framed houses and highly decorated stone mansions.

Many vanished in the Great Fire, it is true, but much survived only to succumb to the Victorian obsession with so-called improvement – streets were widened, whole districts razed. The idea of preserving beautiful early buildings was simply unheard of. German bombers also destroyed a great deal that had survived, but perhaps the worst damage of all was inflicted by architects and planners during the 1960s and 1970s. Far more early buildings were lost in the 1960s and 1970s than in the whole of the Second World War.

Most of the city's churches we see today, though described as by Wren or Hawksmoor, are not really authentic at all – they were rebuilt after bomb damage of various degrees of severity. In many instances the whole church apart from the external walls had to be recreated.

But one church survived the Great Fire, the war, the developers and the 1960s – St Katherine Cree in Creechurch Lane near Houndsditch.

Completed in 1628 (apart from the tower, which dates from more than a century earlier), the church was built on the site of the Augustinian Priory of Holy Trinity, Aldgate. St Katherine Cree was built to minister to the parishioners of Aldgate after the destruction of the priory following the Dissolution of the monasteries. There is some evidence to suggest that the present church was built in the old priory burial ground and may even have been used as a mortuary while the priory still existed.

The church we see today – it takes its curious name, 'Cree', from a corruption of the words 'Christ's Church' – is remarkable not just for its survival against all the odds, but also for the fact that it reveals perhaps better than any other building how London was built one layer upon another.

Inside the main door to the church and a little to the right, visitors will see the top – the capital – of a pillar. Below the capital there is only around two feet of the pillar itself. Why is this?

The answer is that as the floor of the church has been built up bit by bit over the centuries, the pillar has become submerged and now only the top two feet remain to be seen. It is a remarkable example of how quickly layer succeeds layer in an ancient city.

Another oddity about this church can be seen on the wall in the lane outside. The eighteenth-century sundial (it may actually be rather earlier) attached to the wall now tells the time only for a short period each day.

When it was first put here, the sun shone on it for long enough for passers-by to check the time, but as the lane has narrowed over the centuries and higher buildings were erected, the sundial became obsolete.

GRAVEDIGGER'S
COTTAGE

⟡⟡⟡

The Drury Lane area of London now seems rather
grand, but in earlier centuries it was notorious
for crime and prostitution. It was part of a large area
stretching from the notorious region of Seven Dials
just to the north of Covent Garden to the even more
notorious slums surrounding Wych Street that lay to
the south of Drury Lane towards the river.

The whole of Wych Street and the surrounding
area was destroyed early in the twentieth century
to build what is now Southampton Row and the
Aldwych. The medieval houses that the current mon-
olithic buildings replaced would have been the envy
of Europe had they survived, for they all predated the
Great Fire of London. The street pattern here was
medieval, too, but the problem was that the area had
gone down in the world. Formerly grand houses were
subdivided over the centuries as the wealthier moved
out to the suburbs of Park Lane and north towards
Oxford Street. The poor swarmed in Wych Street and
the surrounding streets and landlords spent nothing
on repairs.

One house survives in the area – the famous
so-called Old Curiosity Shop on Portsmouth Street –
but a far less well known and equally curious survivor
can be found on Drury Lane itself.

Here, surrounded by blocks of late Victorian flats

to which the poor of Wych Street were moved, is a tiny park. It was once a burial ground. In fact, it was one of London's most notorious graveyards – bodies were crammed in just below the surface and body-snatchers who stole the recently dead and sold them to medical students were a constant problem.

This problem arose because it was a rule that anyone who died in London had the right to be buried in their parish church, but as London grew this became increasingly difficult until, by the middle years of the nineteenth century, burials meant pressing new bodies in flimsy coffins into already over-filled graves. Eventually things became so bad that gravediggers were encouraged to jump on the coffins to push them down and they were then covered with at best a few inches of soil. The result was appallingly unhygienic and no doubt contributed to levels of disease ensuring that one in three infants among the poor died before they were a year old.

At last, in 1851, London's small graveyards were all closed by an Act of Parliament. As the years passed, the graveyards were emptied of their bones and the headstones often stacked around the edges of the new open space.

At Drury Lane, all signs of the site's former pur-pose have gone – or at least that's how it seems. In fact, two red brick gothic buildings still stand flanking the entrance to the garden. One was the gravedigger's cottage, the other the former mortuary where bodies were kept before burial.

NUMBERS GAME

Many of London's houses conceal remarkable interiors, but none more so than No. 29 Piccadilly. This classical house might easily be taken for a twentieth-century attempt at Georgian architecture; in fact, it is one of the earliest remaining buildings in what was once one of London's most fashionable streets. Piccadilly began to be built up from around 1661, when the land at what is now the eastern end of the street was given to Henry Jermyn, first Earl of St Albans and adviser to Charles II. The Earl is remembered today in the name of nearby Jermyn Street.

Inns and shops were first built overlooking the park and down towards Buckingham Palace (Buckingham House, as it then was) while at the other end were the grand mansions of the rich.

Piccadilly had been known as Portugal Street in honour of Charles II's queen Catherine of Braganza but when Robert Baker, a tailor, made his fortune selling lace collars known as picadils, he bought a big house at the western end of Portugal Street which became known as Piccadilly Hall. The name stuck and soon the whole street became known as Piccadilly and poor Catherine was forgotten.

Nothing survives from the earliest period of development except parts of St James's Church and the core of Burlington House, now the home of the Royal Academy.

Coventry House was built between 1759 and 1762 for Sir Henry Hunloke on the site of an old pub called the Greyhound Inn. By the mid-1760s, the Earl of Coventry had bought a lease on the house and it was he who employed the great architect of the day, Robert Adam, to alter and decorate the interior in the latest fashion. Astonishingly, much of his work still survives to this day, despite numerous (not always sympathetic) owners. Coventry sold the house to Napoleon III's ambassador, Comte de Flahaut de la Billarderie, in 1848. Then, from 1868 to 1978, the house became the St James's Club.

Since then, the house has had a number of commercial owners but still Adam's work survives. If you want to see it, however, you will have to visit Sir John Soane's Museum in Lincoln's Inn Fields where, astonishingly, there are fifty-six exquisite drawings of the interior of Coventry House and many of the rooms they depict are still there just as Adam and his men left them.

One final remarkable thing about Coventry House: it was No. 29 Piccadilly when built, but is now No. 106. The number changed simply because so many magnificent houses in the street were demolished in Victorian times, and later, that the number of houses and shops decreased dramatically. Tragic losses include Devonshire House (the wine cellar became the booking office for Green Park Station), but the magnificent gates from this long-lost mansion can still be seen almost opposite Coventry House and now form part of the Green Park railings.

CHURCHILL IN
A BUCKET

Winston Churchill was famous for many things, not least his remarkable ability to inspire the British people to believe that, however badly things were going in the war, they should not give up hope.

He had a kind of presence, a bulldog quality, remarked on by all his biographers, and he would go to great lengths to show the population of London in particular that, whatever the Germans threw at us, we would get up, dust ourselves down and carry on.

This spirit of determination led to one comic incident which did nothing to lessen Churchill's reputation.

While on a tour of one of London's worst-hit areas during the Blitz, Churchill was surrounded by a huge mob of admirers. He had been talking to a group of firemen and rescue workers, who explained to him that the bombs had not only flattened the surrounding houses but had also damaged the massive Victorian sewers beneath their feet.

Churchill was fascinated by this and immediately asked if he could examine the damaged sewers himself. The only way to do this, explained the firemen, was to be lowered by crane in a large metal bucket. The firemen were convinced Churchill would leave it at that but, ever the eccentric, he immediately demanded that a portable crane be brought over to the huge hole in the ground. He was helped into the large metal bucket suspended from a thick chain and, smiling broadly and making his characteristic victory salute, was lowered into the sewer.

His assistants later explained that he was rather embarrassed on reaching the bottom of the hole to discover that there was absolutely nothing to see, but, rather than be hauled up to the waiting crowd immediately, he sat in the bucket for ten minutes smoking his cigar before shouting to be hauled back up. The crowd, as can be expected, was most impressed.

MOVING HOUSE

O ne of the saddest and strangest stories concerning London houses concerns Lansdowne House,
which originally stood at the south-west corner of
Berkeley Square. A beautiful classical house built by
Robert Adam and completed in 1763, the house had
a large forecourt and its garden stretched across the
whole of the bottom half of Berkeley Square. This
had the added consequence for the Devonshires,
who owned Devonshire House in Piccadilly, that
their house and garden looked out unimpeded across
the garden of Lansdowne House to the garden of the
square itself.

In an act of vandalism now impossible to understand, Westminster City Council decided that keeping
a magnificent house was of far less importance than
encouraging the use of the car, so a plan was hatched
to demolish the whole of the front of the house along
with all the front rooms – all of which had been decorated magnificently by Adam. As a result, a road now
runs where once these priceless rooms were laid out
and the house's former gardens were taken in order
to build two huge office blocks. Meanwhile, a shabby
version of the front of the house was rebuilt thirty feet
back from its original position and the magnificent
drawing room and dining room were shipped off to
American museums.

Today, the sad remains of the house have been turned into the Lansdowne Club. When the club's owners took over from the Petty-Fitzmaurice family, who had owned the house from 1761 until the early 1930s, the club redesigned much of the interior in an Art Deco style, but one or two Adam rooms still remain. Famous residents or owners of the house include at least three prime ministers, including William Pitt the Younger, the artist Beryl Cook and Gordon Selfridge of department store fame.

FRENCH FOR BOLLARDS

❧⋆❧

Bollards are a commonplace in London and many people have noticed how the old cast-iron examples are curiously shaped rather like cannon. Indeed, it was usual among London children playing in the street in Victorian times to refer to the bollards as cannon.

The bizarre truth is that the first bollards installed in London were not made to look like cannon – they actually *were* cannon.

The reason for this is that so many French cannon were captured after the defeat of Napoleon at the Battle of Waterloo in 1815 that the government, rather than waste them, decided they would be useful to prevent the iron-shod wheels of London's tens of thousands of carts and cabs from damaging curbs and corners of buildings.

The captured cannon were driven into the ground and the idea became so popular and useful that, as they corroded or wore out, replicas were made in iron, but still designed to look exactly like the original upended cannon. Today, their tough plastic descendants are still designed to look rather like cannon but, astonishingly, if you wander the south bank near the Globe Theatre you can still see a few of the original French cannon still upright and doing the job for which they were not really designed more than 200 years ago!

HIDDEN MANSION

As the City of London grew in wealth, it became increasingly commercial. As early as the Middle Ages, the wealthiest tried to escape its densely cluttered streets by building mansions along the Strand just outside the western gate – Ludgate. With the exception of the chapel of St John, nothing of these great mansions survives today, but the habit of moving westward continued for centuries until, by the late seventeenth and early eighteenth centuries, fashionable London had moved gradually out to Hyde Park in the west and north beyond what is now Oxford Street to Marylebone Road. Oxford Street had formerly been the Tyburn Road, but the name was changed as it served as an unwelcome reminder that this was the route the condemned took to the Tyburn gallows where Marble Arch now stands.

At first glance, it might appear that all the grand houses between Oxford Street and the Marylebone Road have long vanished, but this is not the case. As the speculative builders moved in and the rich moved even further west and north, some of the great detached mansions were cunningly incorporated into the new terraces for the middle classes.

Nos 100–103 Great Russell Street do not stand out from the houses on either side, but this was once Thanet House, the home of Samuel Johnson's great friend the eccentric Topham Beauclerk (1739–80).

Beauclerk is remembered today only for his friendship with the great author of the first truly comprehensive English dictionary, but in his day he was a well-known wit and man about town. He was perhaps the only man Johnson feared in a contest of wits. In Boswell's *Life of Dr Johnson*, Beauclerk is a central figure. Though querulous and eccentric, he shone in company in which he felt at ease, as we see in Boswell's famous book, and he loved jokes and play. On the downside, he is reputed almost never to have washed, but when he died Johnson said: 'This is a loss the whole nation cannot repair.' Johnson went on to say that: 'No man was ever so free, when he was going to say a good thing, from a look that expressed that it was coming or when he had said it from a look that expressed that it had come.' Johnson concluded that Beauclerk's talents were 'those which he had felt himself most disposed to envy than those of any whom he had known'.

Like another great conversationalist – the twentieth century's Desmond MacCarthy – Beauclerk is now largely forgotten because his great talent lay in the spoken word, rather than writing; only in Boswell do we get a sense of how electrifying Beauclerk could be.

Beauclerk lived at Thanet House in Great Russell Street for many years, but the house had actually existed a century before Beauclerk was born. It was remodelled in the eighteenth century but no doubt retained some deep structures from the earlier house. The list of aristocrats who once lived in this now-forgotten house is impressive: the house gets its name from the Earl of Thanet, who took a 62-year lease in 1693. Sir Thomas Coke, later Viscount Coke, lived here along with the Marquess of Tavistock, the Earl

Bathurst and, intriguingly, Diana Spencer, an ancestor of the late Princess of Wales who was by contemporaneous accounts a talented painter. She eventually married Topham Beauclerk.

By the mid-nineteenth century, Thomas Cubitt, the great-great-grandfather of Camilla, Duchess of Cornwall and wife of the current Prince of Wales, had been employed to remodel the front of the house again, but to this day it echoes its former incarnations.

Another grand house that once stood alone and splendidly isolated is Bourdon House in Davies Street just north of Mayfair.

This five-bay pedimented house faces south today into a garden bordered by Bourdon Street, but if you look carefully you will see that its design is distinct from the houses that now hem it in. It may look like part of a group of houses but it is actually a grand mansion preserved by the Dukes of Westminster who own all the land between here and Belgravia.

PRISON FARE

❧❦❧

L ondon's ancient prisons with their harsh regimes have long vanished, but for those prepared to look carefully in odd places, traces remain. One wall of Marshalsea Prison in Southwark, south London, can still be seen, for example. This prison became famous after Charles Dickens made it the focus of his novel *Little Dorrit*. Dickens knew it well as it was the place where his own father was imprisoned for debt. But among London's least known and strangest prisons was Tothill Fields Bridewell. This was also known at various times as Tothill Fields Prison, Westminster Bridewell and the Westminster House of Correction.

Built in what were then the slums of Westminster, the prison began life in 1618. It was named after Henry VIII's palace on the banks of the River Fleet. Originally one of the king's favourite residences, the palace was handed over to the City of London Corporation by Henry's son Edward VI and it became a prison, or, more precisely, a house of correction, but the name Bridewell became synonymous with prisons generally.

Tothill Bridewell was unique in that prisoners were very rarely whipped or punished violently in any other way. Instead, the prison imposed an absolute rule of silence on its inmates. Anyone who broke the rule had their food ration withdrawn for a day or two.

In 1834, Tothill prison was rebuilt on a new site where Westminster Cathedral now stands at the opposite end of Victoria Street from Westminster Abbey. The rest of the site was covered over with red-brick mansion blocks, many of which survive to this day.

The prison foundations were so extensive that they were used to provide a foundation for the massive cathedral that now stands on the site, but bizarrely Westminster Council decided to keep one part of the prison intact. The prison's stone gateway was moved to Little Sanctuary behind the Middlesex Guildhall and just across the road from Westminster Abbey.

FINAL STEPS

❧✽❧

The area towards the western end of Fleet Street where the Old Bailey (otherwise known as the Central Criminal Court) now stands has a dark and ancient history. The Victorian court buildings were built on part of the site of the old Newgate Prison, at one time one of the most notorious prisons in Europe. Hangings were still a regular public occurrence outside the court until 1868 and the birch was used on inmates who failed to obey the rules. Many of those who were hanged were buried under the floor of Dead Man's Walk, a path between the jail and the old court. Such were the riots that took place on hanging days that a secret tunnel was built between the court and nearby St Sepulchre's Church so that the priest could speak to the condemned before his or her execution without being pelted with rotten eggs and old vegetables by the crowd.

Rebuilt and remodelled numerous times, but especially after the Great Fire, the current buildings date from 1902, but even this relatively modern building retains a gruesome eccentricity; one that is in fact built into its very structure.

The corridor from the condemned cells to the room where executions took place is built in a most odd way. As the condemned steps out of his cell, the ceiling is of a normal height and the walls leave a wide pathway ahead. Within twenty paces, however, the ceiling gradually lowers until the condemned must stoop; the walls close in gradually from the sides until there is barely space for a man to pass. The idea was to remind the condemned that death was closing in on them.

WATERLOO WOMEN

❦

It is a sad truism that if there is a beautiful building or structure in London, there will be someone who would like to redevelop it – a word often used to make destruction sound like something positive.

But one would have thought that a bridge across the Thames that had been celebrated in paintings by Constable and Monet, not to mention being the subject of a fine poem by Thomas Hood, might have escaped. But unfortunately not.

John Rennie's magnificent Georgian Waterloo Bridge, completed in 1817, had nine arches, each separated by pairs of splendid Doric pillars. It was highly decorative and widely admired. London County Council, notoriously blind to the virtues of London architecture, gave the go-ahead to demolish it in the 1930s.

The rather plain, functional bridge that replaced it still stands, but it is a little-known fact that it was largely built by women. They were drafted in between 1939 and 1945, when the new bridge was finally completed.

By the standards of the time, women doing the sort of heavy manual work involved in bridge building was remarkable, but by then the war was on and almost every able-bodied man in the country had been called up.

Yet there was still a great deal of embarrassment about the whole thing if the opening ceremony is anything to go by. The women's contribution was not acknowledged in any of the speeches on the day and none of the women who had worked on the bridge was invited to attend. Labour minister Herbert Morrison said: 'The men who built Waterloo Bridge are fortumate men. They know that, although their names may be forgotten, their work will be a pride and use to London for many generations to come.'

It was all very odd and the mystery deepened when building contractor Peter Lind and Co., who had worked with architect Giles Gilbert Scott on the bridge, went out of business and all their records were destroyed in the early 1980s.

POSTMAN'S PARK

⤜❦⤛

L ondon is famous across the world for its parks.
Indeed, it would be a brave, not to say foolhardy,
politician who suggested we build on any of the
dozens of parks small and large that still exist in every
corner of the capital.

Among the parks, of course, we must include that
peculiarity of London – the square. The idea for the
typical London square began in the late seventeenth
century and lasted well into the nineteenth. Houses
were built round squares that were given over to gardens, gravelled walks and fountains, and many of these
garden squares survive – some would say the fact that
they are not generally open to the public is a great
disadvantage, but actually this exclusivity ensures that
the squares remain havens for wildlife. They are one
of the main reasons London is rich in bird life.

But perhaps the oddest open space in London is
known as Postman's Park.

Situated in the heart of the old City of London, bordered by Aldersgate Street, King Edward Street, Little
Britain and St Martin's Le Grand, the park was once,
like so many open spaces in the city, a burial ground. It
was the churchyard of St Botolph's Aldersgate but the
graves were long ago removed, the gravestones stacked
ignominiously at the edge of the park.

The excuse for clearing the gravestones was that this
area was heavily bombed during the Second World

War. The park encompasses the old graveyards of several churches – but most notably St Leonard, Foster Lane and Christ Church Greyfriars – as well as land made available after the demolition of old houses in Little Britain in 1880.

The park gets its odd name from its popularity among postmen, thousands of whom were formerly employed at the General Post Office headquarters nearby.

But the strangest monument of all in the park was placed here by the great Victorian painter G. F. Watts, whose house – a remarkable curiosity in its own right – still exists in Kensington. Watts was considered an important figure in his day but by the 1960s his work was dismissed by critics and the public alike. A curious story recalls how, in the 1970s, his magnificent painting entitled 'Hope' – now worth millions – was found in a terraced house in south London where it had been used to block an old chimney.

Anyway, for reasons that are now obscure, Watts decided he would pay to affix decorative tiles to a wall in Postman's Park commemorating ordinary Londoners who had done extraordinary things. He was not interested in the rich and the famous, the powerful and the wealthy. Quite the contrary in fact, for the tiles in the park celebrate the selfless deeds of people otherwise now completely forgotten.

Joseph William Onslow, a lighterman, is here commemorated. He was drowned at Wapping in the Thames while trying to save a boy's life.

Or Henry James Bristow who, in tearing off his sister's burning clothes, saved her life, only to lose his own when the flames took hold of him.

Watts had a fairly eccentric personal life. He married the famous actress Ellen Terry when she was just sixteen. He was nearly fifty. The marriage lasted little more than a year before Terry ran off with a younger man.

And it was in 1887, while married to Scottish artist Mary Fraser Tytler (whom Watts had divorced once already and then remarried), that he decided to create his monument to ordinary heroic deeds. When he died in 1904, he had placed thirteen tiles in the wall, but his widow continued to add tiles celebrating the deeds of ordinary people for many years. The last tile added was number fifty-four.

The wall has survived remarkably well and visitors today can sit on a low bench that runs beneath the monuments and contemplate the deeds of those who might otherwise have vanished into the long oblivion of history.

SEWAGE LIGHTING

Many visitors to London are astonished to discover that gas lamps, unchanged from the nineteenth century, still exist in many places – most notably in the streets around St James's Palace and up towards the Palace of Westminster, but perhaps the strangest of these ghostly lights – lights that recall the city of Conan Doyle and Jack the Ripper – is the one still to be found on Carting Lane in the City.

In addition to being beautifully made, this cast-iron lamppost is not powered solely by the mains gas that supplies countless central heating systems across the country; instead it is fuelled by mains gas combined with waste gases produced naturally from the effluent in London's sewers!

Given that methane, one of the most important sewer gases, is highly combustible, it seems odd that only one lamp uses this most useful resource, but no doubt some bright spark will come along and suggest a more widespread use of sewage gas for lighting – it would certainly fit well with current ideas about green renewable energy!

A PIECE OF OLD LONDON BRIDGE

Old London Bridge, which was demolished in 1831, would have been one of the wonders of the world had it had survived until today. Over the 600 years of its existence it survived fires, the collapse of several of the arches on which it was built, and an attack by Wat Tyler during the Peasants' Revolt.

At the height of its fame, the bridge supported around 150 shops, a palace and numerous houses. There was a gatehouse at either end and high above the turrets of the southern gatehouse were the long pikes on which traitors' heads were stuck until they rotted away.

But, of course, the bridge had its drawbacks; the roadway between the houses and shops was very narrow, which impeded the traffic; the bridge's nineteen irregularly shaped arches so impeded the river water that, upstream, the Thames regularly froze in winter and the rush of water in summer through the arches was highly dangerous. Only the most experienced boatman would attempt to 'shoot the bridge'.

Few lamented the final destruction of this marvel, but one or two sentimentalists wanted to keep some memory of a structure that had epitomised London for so long, so at least one of the old stone pedestrian alcoves that once lined the bridge was carefully removed to Victoria Park in east London where to this day it serves as a shelter for pedestrians. Its beautifully cut stone arch and bench reminds us that London Bridge was once the pride of the city.

GOING NOWHERE

❦

During the Blitz, London was heavily bombed in a series of night-time raids that went on for weeks at a time and left large parts of the capital in ruins. The worst part of the bombing was that it was aimed not just at military targets – the railways and the docks, for example – but also at civilian areas.

Londoners quickly got used to the bombing and rather than weakening their resolve to stay in their city, it strengthened it. But the night-time raids meant huge disruption, with thousands of families spending night after night underground in the tube system, in factory and office basements and even, occasionally, in parts of the sewer system.

The bombs uncovered some very odd, long forgotten features of the capital, including stretches of Roman wall that had long lain hidden in the basements of old houses, but one or two other architectural oddities were uncovered by the bombs which have never been explained.

A street of late-Victorian houses in south London was thought to be pretty much like any other similar street in any urban area in the country until one night in 1942 a group of bombers heading back to Germany released their unused bombs just to get rid of them and lighten their aircraft.

The bombs fell on a tall, red-brick Victorian house, scoring a direct hit and blowing out the whole of the front wall, which left the house looking rather like one of those dolls' houses that allow you to remove the front to see what is inside.

When the rescue services and firemen arrived in the street as dawn broke, they were surprised but also relieved to discover that no one appeared to have been in the house when it was hit.

When they began to search more carefully, they realised this was a very odd house indeed. Incredibly, most of the furniture was still standing in the various rooms – the force of the blast appeared to have been taken entirely by the front wall.

All the furniture appeared to be ancient – mid-Victorian in the main. There was nothing odd about that in itself – many people kept their inherited furniture and only rarely bought new things at a time when money was tight and the idea of constantly modernising was still decades in the future. But even by the standards of the time, the furniture and pictures in the house seemed ancient. Shocked neighbours were able to confirm that no one had been seen entering or leaving the house for years, and the curtains were always shut. It was simply assumed that the owners lived elsewhere and couldn't let the house or perhaps just didn't want to. No one had thought anything of it.

In the basement of the house, an old black range was still *in situ* despite the fact that gas cookers were almost universal by this time. Thick dust lay everywhere in the kitchen and it was not the sort of brick and plaster dust one might have expected after an explosion. It was the sort of dust that gathers slowly over many years and only when a room is left entirely undisturbed.

At the back of the kitchen came the strangest thing

of all. An old, thick-planked door led into a brick-vaulted tunnel that led under the garden at the back of the bombed house across another garden and then on to the basement of another, very similar house in the next street.

The tunnel had been blocked just at the point where it should have entered the basement of the other house and the owners of the house to which it led were entirely unaware that a tunnel had been dug between their house and the bombed house nearby.

With war raging and the threat of death ever-present from the bombers, few enquiries were made about this odd house, but eventually someone came forward and claimed to be related to the owners. He insisted the details of the house and its owners were all held by a firm of solicitors in the City, but when enquiries were made it was discovered that the solicitor's office had also been bombed and all the deeds and other paperwork held by the firm had been destroyed. The mystery of the suburban house and the tunnel was never solved.

FOR WHOM THE
BELLS TOLL

S t Sepulchre-without-Newgate isn't as strange as its
name may suggest to modern ears. The 'without'
refers to its position just beyond – i.e. outside – the
old city gate (Newgate).

The church is named after the Church of the Holy
Sepulchre in Jerusalem. What we see today is largely
a late-Georgian remodelling of a much older church
which, like so many of London's churches, was destroyed in the Great Fire of 1666. The Victorians
couldn't keep their hands off the church either, so
much that is not Georgian is late nineteenth century.

Apart from its name, what makes St Sepulchre
fascinating is that it still retains the old hand bell
that was rung outside the condemned cell at the old
Newgate Prison. On execution days the bell would be
rung and the condemned led out to a cart that would
then carry them along the Tyburn Road (now Oxford
Street) via St Giles near Seven Dials and then finally
to Tyburn (now Marble Arch) where the execution by
hanging would take place.

But these were not always gruesome occasions. Very
unpopular prisoners, it is true, were pelted with dead
cats and rotten vegetables, but there were also prisoners who were heroes and they would be cheered all the
way from Newgate Prison to Tyburn. In fact, so popular were some of the condemned that the authorities

had to marshal a large contingent of solders to guard the prison tumbrels in case the mob attacked them in an attempt to rescue the condemned. As one wag put it: 'The heroes of the day were often on good terms with the mob, and jokes were exchanged between the men who were going to be hanged and the men who deserved to be.'

The old bell now sits in a glass case but no doubt the vicar will allow you to hear its ghostly sound if you ask him.

Another curious custom observed at St Sepulchre's was the presentation of a nosegay to every criminal on the way to execution at Tyburn. No doubt the practice had its origin in some kindly feeling for the poor unfortunates who were so soon to bid farewell to life. One of the last who received a nosegay from the steps of St Sepulchre's was John Rann, alias 'Sixteen-String Jack', who was hanged in 1774 for robbing the Revd Dr Bell of his watch and eighteen pence in money, in Gunnersbury Lane on the road to Brentford. Sixteen String Jack wore the flowers in his button-hole as he rode to the gallows. This was witnessed by John Thomas Smith, who describes the scene in his book *Nollekens and His Times*:

> I remember well, when I was in my eighth year, Mr Nollekens calling at my father's house, in Great Portland Street, and taking us to Oxford Street, to see the notorious Jack Rann, commonly called Sixteenstring Jack, go to Tyburn to be hanged. The criminal was dressed in a pea-green coat, with an immense nosegay in the button-hole, which had been presented to him at St Sepulchre's steps; and his nankeen small-clothes, we were told, were tied at each

knee with sixteen strings. After he had passed, and
Mr Nollekens was leading me home by the hand, I
recollect his stooping down to me and observing, in
a low tone of voice, 'Tom, now, my little man, if my
father-in-law, Mr Justice Welch, had been high constable, we could have walked by the side of the cart all
the way to Tyburn.'

THE LOST GRAVEYARD

❦

Visitors to London don't often go to Fulham, except perhaps to see the remains of the wonderful old Tudor Bishop's Palace by the river. The rest of this suburb is peculiarly lacking in interesting or historic buildings, despite the fact that centuries ago there were several splendid houses here. There is, however, an exception – one very strange survivor in this otherwise unexceptional borough.

Walk along Queen's Elm Parade and you will pass high Victorian walls which seem to enclose nothing – or at least nothing requiring an entrance. Even local residents give the walls and the land they enclose almost no thought. Behind them, a smallish plot of ground has been largely unused and only rarely entered since as long ago as 1885.

The story begins in 1815 when the Society of Jews paid £400 for this small patch of land in which they could bury their dead. At the time it was surrounded entirely by farms and meadows, which were famous for skylarks. By 1885, the burial ground was full. Around 700 people are buried here. Once it was full, the gates were closed except to the relatives of the dead, but gradually over the following century the relatives of the dead themselves died and the place was largely forgotten. It remains an enigma today – unvisited and entirely inaccessible.

But there is one consolation — it is said to be hugely popular with songbirds, who build their nests here in the quiet, undisturbed by humans or their dogs or cats.

SARACEN'S HEADS

A curious tale surrounds the popularity of pubs in London (and elsewhere) with the name 'Saracen's Head'. This ancient name dates back to the last of the crusades in the late thirteenth century when returning soldiers found themselves without employment and in many cases set up as inn keepers. Among these veterans there was a feeling that their final defeat was somehow rather ignominious so, to make it less embarrassing, those who set up pubs and inns made sure that the Saracen's Head part of the painting on their signs was huge and monstrous. The idea was that such great and terrifying creatures were so awesome that no ordinary mortal ever had a hope of defeating them. The returning soldiers had effectively set up a series of advertisements explaining their defeat as something that showed no discredit to them at all!

BRIDGE TOO FAR

꧁⁂꧂

The curiously named Thousand Pound Pond is
one of the delights of the grounds of Kenwood
House in north London. No one knows for sure
where the pond gets this curious name, but the best
guess is that in the early 1920s, when preservationists
were desperately trying to save as much as possible of
this part of Hampstead Heath from the developers,
they persuaded Lord Mansfield to sell some thirty-
two acres, including the woodland and lakes we see
today, but Mansfield demanded a staggering £1,000
per acre. The pond covers about one acre of the land so
it might have seemed logical to refer to it from then
on as the Thousand Pound Pond.

The pond itself was made in the late eighteenth
century – certainly it was complete by 1791 and its
creation was part of that huge eighteenth-century
enthusiasm for landscaping.

But the oddest thing about the lake is the beautiful
bridge that has long been admired by visitors. Even
today when people come to admire the woodland
walks and visit the beautiful house with its priceless
collection of pictures, they inevitably think to complete their visit by crossing the white bridge at the end
of the pond.

Visitors soon realise, however, that this is completely impossible. The bridge is a sham and is just

a few inches in width. It was created when the pond was made simply to provide an attractive view and is virtually two dimensional, a cardboard (or timber) cut-out.

MPS' SNUFFBOX

T he House of Commons has long been famous
for its rather eccentric practices. Until recently,
for example, any MP wishing to interrupt a certain
kind of debate had to don a top hat before rising to
his feet to speak.

The building in which MPs do their work is perhaps
equally eccentric. Because it was designed by the great
– and obsessive – high priests of Gothic, Augustus
Pugin and Charles Barry, it had to have a very real
medieval flavour. This was achieved in part at least by
including sword rests here and there in various rooms,
even though by the time the Commons was built in
the 1830s, swords had long become an anachronism.

The building's designers also forgot that any building by the side of the river is likely to subside – which
is why the Palace of Westminster (as the two Houses
of Parliament are jointly known) sinks a centimetre or
two into the mud each year.

So eccentric was the design of the building that it
includes vast numbers of tiny hidden voids under the
floors, between the walls and behind the wainscot. The
result is that there is no accurate and complete map of
the underlying structure of the building, which in turn
means that every attempt to get rid of the more than
half a million mice that infest the palace has failed.

Many visitors wonder why, after wartime damage,
the House of Commons was deliberately built with

too few seats for all the MPs. The answer reveals the extraordinary power of one man: Winston Churchill. It is impossible today to imagine that one man, even if he happened to be prime minister, could insist that Parliament be deliberately made too small and get away with it. But this is exactly what Churchill did. He knew that it is rare for the house ever to be full since attendance at debates is rarely compulsory for MPs. Given that there would usually only be a relatively small number of MPs in the House at any one time, he thought a small chamber would ensure that it always looked relatively busy.

COAL CELLAR CRYPT

Vast amounts of London's history remain hidden beneath later buildings. The city is so multi-layered that in places you would need to dig down two or three metres to reach the level on which the Romans lived. This is especially true in the City proper, which was inhabited for so much longer than outlying regions such as the Strand and, east of the city, the hamlets beyond the Tower of London.

But Fleet Street runs the city a close second in this respect. Just outside the western gate of the city along the river were several large convents and priories. Blackfriars Bridge, which crosses the River Thames at the point roughly where the old River Fleet would have run into it, echoes in its name the foundation of the black friars, or Black Frères, Dominican friars who established their priory here in 1276.

A little further to the west, along Fleet Street, the Whitefriars (who wore white habits) established their Carmelite priory in 1253. Until the end of the nineteenth century it was assumed that, following the destruction of both the Blackfriars and Whitefriars priories in 1540, nothing of them remained.

Then, during building work, a remarkable discovery was made. Beneath later buildings in what is now Magpie Alley, workmen discovered the almost perfectly preserved Whitefriars crypt.

Though preserved, the crypt was moved several metres from its original site and an office block was built on top. But if you go down the steps at the end of Magpie Alley you can see the crypt which, absurdly, is now contained in a glass box.

ARM'S LENGTH

Few people under the age of fifty now remember in any detail the old coinage system that was replaced in the early 1970s when Britain became decimalised. The old system was a nightmare for foreigners used to coinage being based on multiples of ten. There were twenty shillings to the pound and each shilling could be split into twelve pennies. There were crown coins (five shillings), half-crown coins (worth two shillings and sixpence) and even threepenny pieces.

Many other equally strange coins, including the farthing (a quarter of a penny), had only gone out of circulation in the 1950s.

But, just as strange as the monetary system, was the old system of measurement and in many parts of London this ancient system is still reflected in the width and height of houses, as well as the layout of squares and parks.

It is astonishing that, until well into the twentieth century, houses were built using the old imperial system of measurement that was based on the ninth-century furlong – from old English *furh* (meaning furrow) and *lang* (meaning long). This was the measurement of an agricultural strip. Most Victorian and Georgian buildings in London are therefore constructed on the basis of a system of measurement that predates the Norman conquest.

For the uninitiated, a furlong is 660 feet long. An

acre is one furlong long and one chain (66 feet) wide. Smaller divisions (that would have been used for house plots) were the rod, pole and perch. Four rods were equal to one chain and one chain in London was used to measure four house fronts. Builders' rules were based on the fathom, which was the distance between two outstretched arms.

When modern metric measurement systems began to be used in London, the old unity was broken, but many houses remain to show us how the influence of the Saxons on London buildings lasted more than a thousand years.

A magnificent example of the old measurement system in action can be seen in Belgrave Square, which was laid out to measure precisely ten chains by ten chains. As it has never been altered since it was completed in the first half of the nineteenth century, it still baffles modern surveyors!

TOMB RAIDER

⌘

The Victorians, it has often been said, were obsessed by death. Partly this was because in Victorian times the influence of the monarch was all-pervasive. When the Queen's Consort Prince Albert died from typhoid in 1861, the queen went into mourning for the rest of her life – and what a long life it was.

The queen wore black every day and gradually so did her subjects, as this was a time when the public slavishly aped the monarchy and criticism of the royal family was almost unthinkable – which was a remarkable turnaround from the days of the Regency early in the nineteenth century when the Prince Regent was regularly pilloried in the newspapers and by cartoonists such as Gillray and Rowlandson.

Queen Victoria's obsession with death led to a whole new style of architecture. The gloom of Gothic which had been exciting and new in the 1830s when Parliament was rebuilt in a Gothic style gradually became a dead style, leaden and sterile and weighing heavily on social and civic life.

This was reflected as much if not more than anywhere else in Victorian cemeteries. When London parish churches were finally forbidden to bury any more bodies in their overcrowded graveyards, large municipal cemeteries opened in the suburbs and the extra space encouraged those who were half in love with death to build ever bigger and more elaborate monuments to those who had died.

Kensal Green Cemetery, which was very fashionable after it opened in 1833, has some wonderfully elaborate Gothic tombs; likewise the Egyptian tombs of Highgate Cemetery. But perhaps the strangest tomb of all is hidden away in a small churchyard on the edge of London.

In Pinner Parish Church – the thirteenth-century church of John the Baptist – there is a giant stone tomb that looks rather like an arrowhead. There is an arch that runs through the base of the structure to create this shape, which has elaborate ironwork and the words 'I bide my time' engraved on its surface.

Perhaps the oddest thing about the monument, apart from its sheer size, is that protruding from either side of the vertical stone face are what look like the two ends of a coffin!

The tomb was built by the horticultural writer John Claudius Loudon for his father, William, who died in 1809. John's mother Agnes died in 1841 and was also buried here.

The story behind the tomb is at least as curious as the tomb itself. Apparently William and Agnes Loudon had inherited a large amount of money through a family will, but that money could only come to them if they were buried above ground. The elaborate tomb was thus in part at least a way to keep the money in the family!

John Loudon was a fascinating character who wrote several important horticultural books and was an important influence on the development of that most characteristic London feature, the garden square. He also invented the curved iron glazing bar that made

Paxton's Crystal Palace possible. An opium addict, he was in the process of designing Southampton cemetery when he died penniless in London in 1843. He is buried in Kensal Green Cemetery in a tomb that is considerably less elaborate than the one he built for his parents.

HORSE HIGH

Horses have never quite disappeared from London's streets. Until well into the 1950s, milk was delivered by pony cart in poorer parts of the city. Until well into the 1970s, the totters, or rag and bone men, still used ponies to pull their carts through the streets and the cry 'Any old iron' was, if you like, an early plea for recycling. The totters also made a good living collecting scrap metal and their income was boosted at least in part because they had no transport fuel bills to pay. This benefit was especially apparent when petrol prices began to soar in the early 1970s.

The totters and milk vans had gone by the 1990s, but one group of horses still had a decade and more to add their splendour to the streets as at least two of London's oldest brewers retained their massive beer drays and the shire horses that pulled them. They did this partly because horses and colourful carts were a good advertisement for their beer, but also because delivering in this way to local pubs owned by breweries such as Young's in Wandsworth and Fuller's in Chiswick made economic sense. Young's and Fuller's finally gave up on their horses in the early years of this century, but horses can still be seen in the form of police horses, a common sight on the streets of central London to this day and their existence explains a feature of central London that baffles Londoners and visitors alike. Traffic lights across the capital, as elsewhere, always have a separate post on which are fixed the lights that tell pedestrians it is safe to cross.

The button that pedestrians press is sensibly about a metre from the ground, but where horses still cross a duplicate button exists around seven feet from the ground. Visitors sometimes notice these buttons and joke that some Londoners must be giants, but the devices exist simply to allow police riders to stop the traffic without the need to dismount and press the lower button.

DOG LICK REPLICA

❧❧❧

One of the strangest sights in south London is the statue of a dog licking out a pot which stands on a replica cast-iron bracket at the top of a post at the corner of Union Street and Blackfriars Road. The golden-brown metal dog with its head half in a black pot is a reminder of a famous sign that once stood on a bracket outside J. W. Cunningham's shop at 196 Blackfriars Road.

This splendid shop was in business from the late eighteenth century until 1931 when the town planners decided to demolish most of the buildings. The original handmade brass-and-timber dog and pot was preserved and is now in the Southwark Museum. It and the replica that now stands on its post are a reminder not just of a famous sign, but also of the fact that London businesses were famous for erecting eccentric or elaborate signs to draw attention to their businesses. A good sign would soon be the talk of the town and would draw customers from far and wide.

Clockmakers would put clocks outside their businesses – one famous clock and watchmaker's shop in Acton, west London, went one better and put a huge clock around 6 feet square above his door. The shop itself was only about 12 feet wide!

Wooden signs showing a Native American chief were popular outside tobacconists' shops (the idea that they smoked peace pipes seems to have been the connection) and large wooden fish might be hoisted above the doors of fishmongers and fishing tackle shops.

But the dog and pot is also famous because it was seen by Charles Dickens every night as he walked home as a boy from the Bottle Blacking factory just off the Strand. He mentions the sign at length in a letter to his first biographer John Forster in 1847. Dickens would have been saddened at the destruction of almost every building he would have known on that walk but he might also have been surprised that the golden dog he knew is now a curious shade of brown!

TUMMY RUMBLINGS

⸎

The St Pancras New Church on Euston Road was the most expensive church ever built in London (apart from St Paul's) at the time of its completion in 1822.

Anyone who has visited the Acropolis of Athens will immediately notice something odd about this church: on one side of its exterior (the side facing the Euston Road) it appears to be an exact replica of the Ionic Temple of the Erechtheum. The porch, as in Athens, is held up by six caryatids that guard the entrance to the vaults.

The Latin term *caryatid* (from the Greek *korai*, meaning maidens) has come to refer to any sculpted female figure used as a support in architecture, but the name probably derives from the city state of Sparta in the Greek Peloponnese. There was a temple here to Artemis Caryatis (Artemis of the Walnut Tree) and here each year the goddess was celebrated by young women dancing.

When the stone maidens were delivered to the replica Erechtheum on the Euston Road, however, their usually serene expressions may have become rather perturbed.

Charles Rossi, who made them from terracotta for Greek Revival architects William and Henry Inwood, delivered them to the site and then made a terrible discovery – they had been made a few inches too tall to fit beneath the porch they were supposed to support.

Perhaps today the lawyers would have become involved and the porch would have been completely rebuilt to rectify the mistake. Rossi had a much better, quicker and cheaper idea.

He simply cut a short section from the midriff of each statue and then fitted the upper and lower portions back together. It was just enough to make the statues fit into the places where they have remained for the past 190 years.

But the eagle-eyed will notice that these elegant and beautiful figures are strangely out of proportion, with long legs and surprisingly short torsos!

UGLY QUEENS

❧✿❧

The arrival of William of Orange in England and the exile of King James II famously solved the problem of Catholics inheriting the British crown. William was reasonably popular with the British, as was Anne, his sister-in-law, who reigned following William's death in 1702.

But there was always a sense among the traditionally irreverent British that these foreign princes were not to be taken too seriously. And the habit of mocking the monarchy became a key feature of much of British life from the arrival of George I after Anne's death in 1714. George had only one real claim to the throne – he was Anne's closest living Protestant relative.

George was mocked by the British public because his English was poor and he was constantly going home to Germany. Many people thought he was illiterate and stupid but this had more to do with his rather wooden public persona than any genuine lack of intelligence. But if George was mocked, so too were his son and grandson, George II and George III.

By the time we reach George IV, the British had largely forgotten the German origins of their royal family and they were so used to their monarchs behaving immorally with strings of mistresses that they didn't worry about that either. But when George IV divorced his wife Caroline of Brunswick, the public was outraged.

It was said that George, then Prince of Wales, had only married Caroline because she was rich and his gambling debts were huge, but in those pre-photographic days George had to agree to marry Caroline without ever having actually met her.

George had seen paintings of his bride to be but court painters of the time were employed to flatter their sitters rather than strive for accuracy, so when George met Caroline for the first time in 1795, he was absolutely horrified. She was so ugly he wanted to call the marriage off, but of course this was impossible. It was the start of a terrible relationship that made George immensely unpopular. If he had stayed married to Caroline but enjoyed the favours of an endless series of mistresses, few would have complained – after all, this is what monarchs traditionally did. Caroline's role was to provide a male heir but even that she failed to do. Her daughter was born in 1796 by which time George was refusing even to see her. George eventually became king in 1820 and Caroline died, still his queen, in 1821. He had tried to divorce her soon after becoming king, but this was extremely difficult, even for a monarch. George tried to find proof of adultery in order to justify the separation – absurd and hypocritical since his own adulterous relationships had long been the talk of the town. But George had another even more insurmountable difficulty – prior to marrying Caroline, he had already married someone else! He is the only bigamist king in British history (although his first marriage, to Maria Fitzherbert, was judged invalid on the grounds that she was a Roman Catholic and the king had not given permission for it to go ahead).

George failed in his attempts to divorce Caroline partly because she was so popular with the British public, who took her side largely because they so hated her husband. At the coronation she stood outside with her supporters who then jeered her husband. It had all the makings of a farce.

The problem was solved a few months after the row had reached its peak when Caroline died.

It is from this highly volatile relationship that one of London's strangest tales stems. George so hated Caroline that after her death he insisted that the house she had lived in on Blackheath, south London after their estrangement should be razed to the ground. He wanted the demolition carried out in such a way that no trace should remain of the house. It was thought he had been successful, but in the 1990s a tiny part of the house was rediscovered. If you want to see where Caroline once bathed at Montagu House in Blackheath you still can – the sunken bath with its short flight of steps is still there in today's Greenwich Park.

GREATHEAD'S TUNNEL

⁓⊱◈⊰⁓

There is a long history of digging tunnels under the River Thames, and one reason for this is that London is built on clay, which is a relatively stable material for digging.

The first Thames tunnel was dug by Cornish miners between Wapping and Rotherhithe in the eighteenth century, but after water broke through on several occasions it was abandoned.

The first successful tunnel was built by Isambard Kingdom Brunel and his father Marc among others. It was dug between 1825 and 1841, again between Wapping and Rotherhithe. It succeeded after the invention by the Brunels and an engineer called Thomas Cochrane of a tunnel shield that allowed the tunnel to be dug inch by inch and then immediately shored up behind the cutting face.

Though it cost far more than it should have, the Wapping tunnel was hugely popular and a tourist attraction in its day. Even Queen Victorian paid a visit. The tunnel still exists but is now used by the London Overground.

Another, altogether stranger tunnel was dug between the Tower of London and the south side of the river, and this largely forgotten tunnel explains a curious brick-built, circular building at Tower Hill. This is all that remains above ground of Mr Greathead's Tunnel.

James Greathead (1844–96) was a brilliant civil engineer who helped perfect the kind of tunnelling machine used by the Brunels for their earlier tunnel. Greathead's innovations are still the basis for modern tunnelling equipment – but the tunnel he built at an astonishingly low cost is now used to carry mains water across the river, and all that remains of his efforts is this curious brick pill box.

BOY ON A BASKET

In Panyer Alley near St Paul's Underground Station can be found one of London's most delightful and overlooked monuments. Known as 'The Panyer Boy', it has been in this area since the 1680s and, wonderful though its survival is, we must also lament that as a result of continual redevelopment the Panyer Boy has been moved and repositioned up and down the same street at least four times. The panyer boy can currently be found on a wall close to the steps down into St Paul's Underground Station.

The boy in the carving appears to be sitting on what looks like a bread basket (or 'pannier'), but the stone is now eroded so it is difficult to be sure. It could be a bale of wool or even straw, and at some stage the carving was locally known as 'pick my toe' because if you look at it from the right angle it looks as if the boy has simply sat down on the nearest comfortable object and begun picking at one of his toes.

The inscription beneath the boy tells us nothing about what the boy is doing. It reads:

When ye have sought the City round,
Yet this is the highest ground.

This is baffling because this street is definitely not the highest point in the city, and we can be pretty sure that there is a link between the sculpture and Panyer

Alley because, so far as we know, the little boy has always been somewhere in the alley and we also know that bread was sold here in medieval times. There was also a bread market in nearby St Martin's le Grand. ·

But then there is still the oddity of that reference to 'the highest ground'. Panyer Alley may not be the highest spot in the city today but then, like so much of the old city, the area has been rebuilt so many times that the ground has fallen and so has all the ground round about.

It may be that at the time the boy was made, this was the highest ground in the city or nearly so – certainly in the mid-nineteenth century it was believed to be at least the second highest point after the standard on nearby Cornhill.

After the Great Fire, when almost all the city was rebuilt in brick, Panyer Alley was a street of fine houses with shops underneath, and we know that the Panyer Boy was affixed to one of these houses. Later houses in the street before the coming of office blocks were demolished in the late nineteenth century, but when the new buildings went up the Panyer Boy was re-embedded in the new wall.

The simplest explanation is probably that he is connected with the bread sellers formerly found here and perhaps also there is a connection with an old pub, The Panyer, that stood halfway along the alley.

STARING DEVILS

The Church of St Peter upon Cornhill has suffered, like so many London churches, from the encroachments of greedy developers over the years, but in the 1890s the rector and churchwardens managed to put a stop to the work of one unscrupulous builder.

A new building was being put up next to the church and work was going well when the rector noticed that the architect of the new building had stolen a foot or more of land owned by the church. He protested, threatened legal action and all work came to a halt.

The architect was furious and insisted that a foot was neither here nor there and that any changes to the building at this stage would be complicated and horribly expensive, but the rector would not budge and so the architect had to redraw his plans and give back the stolen strip of land.

By law, of course, there was nothing he could do, but he found another way to exact revenge. He decorated his new buildings with terracotta devils that to this day stare down on the entrance to the church. One of the devils was even deliberately carved so that its face was exactly like that of the rector with whom the architect had fallen out.

TEMPERANCE CUPS

❧✦❧

The Victorian middle and upper classes were obsessed with the idea that the working classes were somehow a race part. Social divisions in the nineteenth century were extraordinarily rigid and only very rarely through talent – as in the case of Charles Dickens – would the lower classes enter the glittering world of money and status.

The Victorian era was also one in which Christianity became more militant. The cosy Georgian world of the Anglican Church where the poor accepted their place and the role of the clergy was to drink port and go to each other's houses for luncheon was long gone. The church was keen to hunt down sin and they saw alcohol as the chief corrupter of men's lives. It never occurred to them that the only respite the poor had from their harsh lives was the pub and the alcohol served there.

So Victorian London was a curious mix of huge, glamorous, brightly lit public houses (called gin palaces), which were built to encourage drinking, and the clergy, who denounced the evils of drink from the pulpit wherever they could.

One eccentric move by the Metropolitan Drinking Fountain Association to try to stop people drinking alcohol was to install elaborate stone fountains next to or opposite the huge new gin palaces. How they could have been so naive as to think that water was ever likely to be a substitute for alcohol is difficult now to understand, but think it they did.

A few of these curious drinking fountains still remain, but very few retain the tin cups on chains that were once so characteristic of them. One well-preserved example does still exist, however, and it is built into the railing of St Sepulchre's Church near Holborn Viaduct and close to one of the best-preserved examples of the gin palace – the Viaduct Tavern.

The drinking fountain has not one, but two old tin cups hanging from chains. They have been made redundant as, presumably for reasons of hygiene, the water was long ago turned off.

PET MEMORIAL

❧⚜❧

Burying one's pet with an elaborate headstone and the kind of inscription one would normally expect to see on a human memorial was to a large extent an invention of the Victorians. Famously obsessed by death, the Victorians turned funerals in general into an art form, with elaborately plumed black horses pulling engraved glass hearses draped in mourning black.

Death became something of enormous sentimental interest and this was matched by an increase in sentimentality when it came to dogs, cats, parrots and budgerigars. Thus pet cemeteries began to appear across London – a famous one exists tucked away on the north side of Kensington Gardens – but care for pets also led to a curious feature of many parks. Both Green Park and St James's Park until recently had lampposts at the bottom of which were tiny stone drinking troughs with a miniscule lead pipe leading into them. The idea was that passing dogs (and perhaps cats) would always be able to have a drink. Presumably the rabbits that lived in Kensington Gardens until the mid-1960s were also able to enjoy a refreshing sip at these odd little watering holes.

CUTTING THE RIBBON

Until 1917, one of London's most picturesque streets was Cloth Fair in the delightfully named ward of Farringdon Within (meaning within the old City walls). This narrow street runs from Little Britain to Middle Street, a distance of just 150 yards, and along the side of the old Church of St Bartholomew the Great, one of London's least-altered and most ancient churches.

In 1917, almost all the old houses in Cloth Fair were pulled down. Just one seventeenth-century house survives today but it has been so over-restored that you might easily think it modern. But Cloth Fair still has a curious tale to tell for, tiny though it is, it was, until around 1910, a liberty.

A liberty is a very peculiar area of land that in medieval times was under the control of the king, and that control devolved either to a bishop or local nobleman. For centuries thereafter the area designated a liberty had its own rules and system of governance, and was exempt from any restrictions or rules implemented via local government in the area surrounding it.

This led to some very odd situations. In south London at Southwark, for example, the Clink Prison and much of the area surrounding it was run as a sort of personal fiefdom by the Bishop of Winchester, who used his powers to run and profit from a series of brothels.

Cloth Fair was even more remarkable as it survived the Local Government Act of 1888 that abolished many of the remaining liberties up and down the country. Then, in 1910, Cloth Fair, which until that date closed its gates against the world each night, decided it needed street lighting and to be connected to the sewage system. It did not have enough money to do this on its own. The only way to modernise was to join the surrounding local council. The Liberty of Cloth Fair then ceased to exist, but the delightful narrow road can still be found, with its ancient church and the former home of poet John Betjeman.

GRASSHOPPER RESCUE

❦

Visitors to London are often baffled by a large golden grasshopper that sits on top of what used to be the City's most important commercial building – the Royal Exchange.

The present mid-Victorian building was altered in 2001 but enough of the original fabric survives to make the building well worth a visit. But what of the grasshopper?

Well, the Royal Exchange was founded by financier Sir Thomas Gresham in 1565. Gresham was a brilliant banker who wanted somewhere in London for merchants to meet to buy and exchange goods and services. For more than a century after it was built, the Royal Exchange specifically excluded stockbrokers on the grounds that they were loud, uncouth and untrustworthy, which is a curious reflection on how little has changed since those days.

The first notable member of the Gresham family enters history in the 1200s. He was Sir Roger Gresham and the story goes that he was abandoned as a baby in a field in Norfolk and would have died but for the fact that the noise of a cricket singing attracted the attention of a passer-by, who came into the field and found him.

The golden grasshopper commemorates that family legend and it also appears as part of the crest of Gresham College in Norfolk, which was founded in 1555 by another Gresham – Sir John.

The school was set up using funds and income from property stolen by Henry VIII from the Augustinian Priory at nearby Beeston Regis.

The story of the boy saved by the noisy grasshopper is a rather nice one, but it is more likely that the grasshopper connection is rather more prosaic. The grasshopper is almost certainly just a visual pun on the Middle English word for grass – *gres* (as in Gresham).

HIGH DAYS AT
THE HOTEL

❧⟨✦⟩❧

The early 1960s saw the destruction of one of the capital's most marvellous landmarks, but it was a landmark with a difference and one little known outside a relatively small circle.

The Cavendish Hotel had been based in three adjoining Regency houses in Jermyn Street (and the corner of Duke Street) since at least the mid-nineteenth century. Then, in 1902, a young woman who had already made a name for herself as a cook heard that the lease of the hotel was about to run out and that the proprietor wanted to retire. The young woman decided this was her chance.

Rosa Lewis was born in London's East End in 1867. She went to a local board school and started work as a kitchen maid aged twelve. She was very good-looking, very quick-witted and learned fast. Soon she was working as a cook in her own right. She worked for Mrs Randolph Churchill and then moved to France where she became famous for her menus.

Back in England a few years later, she found herself much in demand. Edward VII, with whom she was rumoured to have had an affair, insisted she cook for him and she travelled all over the country with Edward and a team of chosen girls to do it. While working for Winston Churchill's mother, she was pestered in the kitchen by the young Winston until, goaded beyond endurance, she shouted 'Hop it, Copper Knob' at him. For Rosa Lewis that was mild language, for she was famously and hilariously foul-mouthed.

Even in the days of her wealth and fame she continued to go to Covent Garden market each morning at 5 a.m. to buy the freshest fruit and vegetables. But her fame as an extraordinary character as well as an extraordinary cook really began to spread when she took over the Cavendish Hotel.

Within a year, the establishment was attracting a rich and aristocratic clientele, despite the fact that it was shabby and filled with eccentric items of furniture. One guest recalled that it was like a magnificent but rather dirty and run-down country house. Huge sofas were combined with old rugs and painted floor boards, rickety old pieces of furniture leant against crooked walls and dogs seemed to be asleep everywhere. Rosa divided part of the hotel into suites where the very rich and well connected, including the king, could entertain in private.

The aristocrats who stayed at the Cavendish became Rosa's friends and she would accompany them to the opera – an extraordinary thing in early-twentieth-century London when servants were usually treated as if they simply did not exist. Her admirers, including Lord Ribblesdale who was devoted to her, regularly sent her cartloads of flowers, which she promptly sent on to any of her friends who happened to be in hospital or prison.

Anyone down on their luck would be allowed to stay free of charge – sometimes for years – and she would charge their bills to her super-rich clients who barely seemed to notice. If they did complain she would say, 'Don't worry about that; it will all come out in the wash.'

She herself drank nothing but champagne and was utterly fearless in defence of those she liked, but she would terrify those she didn't take to with a string of the foulest expletives. As she grew older, she grew more eccentric and would deliberately mispronounce her guests' names or pretend she had mistaken them for someone else.

Rosa became so wealthy she was able to buy a country house but, having thrown her drunken husband out of the hotel soon after it opened, she never remarried, preferring instead the company of her lifelong friend Edith.

Much of the hotel was decorated with old empty Jeroboams of champagne, their labels signed by the great and the good. Rosa also loved going to the sale-rooms and would buy ridiculously impractical items – a stuffed rhinoceros, a set of huge Gobelin tapestries (which turned out to be fakes) and, maddest of all, a huge set of gates from Dorchester House in Park Lane when it was demolished in the 1920s.

Rosa Lewis's Cavendish was said to be the most entertaining place in London. It even housed a full-blown aristocratic prostitute, who stayed free of charge provided she continued to provide gentlemen's services. If any of Rosa's guests decided not to use her services and instead picked a girl up in Piccadilly, Rosa would shout at them when they returned to the hotel: 'We'll get the doctor to look at your winkle in the morning.'

'She always did it when there were others milling about in the hall,' recalled one of her regulars, 'to maximise the embarrassment and teach you never to do it again!'

When Rosa died in her sleep in 1952, aged eighty-five, the hotel carried on for another decade, but changing tastes and changing times led to a decline in the hotel's popularity and it was forced to close in 1962. The new owners promised they would at least retain the buildings (or their facades – the hotel was composed of several beautiful old houses that had been knocked together), but they went back on their word and the old hotel was razed to the ground to be replaced by the infinitely dull Cavendish Hotel that stands on the site today.

THE VANISHED INN

Barnard's Inn, which was founded in 1252 as a school for law students, once took up a large area of land between Fetter Lane and Holborn. A seventeenth-century timber-framed and jettied front looked out over Fetter Lane for centuries, but bombs and redevelopment destroyed these once magnificent buildings long ago and it is easy to imagine that nothing of Barnard's Inn survives.

In fact, through a narrow alleyway off Holborn there still stands, almost completely surrounded by ugly modern buildings, yet largely intact, the late fourteenth-century hall of this ancient Inn of Court. Astonishingly, much of its original fabric survives, including the magnificent crown-post and collar-purling roof structure and sixteenth-century linenfold panelling. The elaborate timber structure that holds up the roof was typical of many late-medieval London houses, but this is the only remaining example in London.

Even more extraordinary is the fact that the chalk-and-tile wall at the southern end of the building is almost certainly Roman work.

Barnard's Inn as a lawyers' inn is long gone, but their building has provided a home for Gresham College since the early 1990s and is now used for meetings and dinners. Gresham College is itself a remarkable survivor, having organised free lectures and talks in London for more than four centuries.

MOHEGAN MEMORIES

It's a sad fact that Britain's centuries of empire-building caused a great deal of suffering and misery across the globe. Of course, it is easy to judge the past rather unfairly using the standards of the present, though London still has odd reminders of individuals' stories that remind us of the human cost of empire.

It is believed that the body of the Native American princess Pocahontas lies under a car park in Gravesend, for example. Born in Virginia in 1595, she married Englishman John Rolfe and returned to London with him. She was fêted and became something of a celebrity, but later generations have felt unease at how she was presented as a civilised savage and applauded for the extent to which she had adopted English manners and dress.

By contrast, another Native American was far less complacent.

In 1736, a little over a century after Pocahontas died in London aged twenty-one, Mahomet Weyonomon, a Mohegan chief from Connecticut, came to England to try to persuade King George II that English settlers had illegally taken land lived on by Mohegan for thousands of years.

How Mahomet must have regretted his people's decision to help the first settlers in New England. It was his tribe that showed them how to get through the bitter winters of North America, and without their help the first colonists would undoubtedly have all died.

However, officials in London refused him an audience with the king and the matter was referred to an obscure commission, where it was no doubt put to the bottom of a very large pile of other, 'more important' matters.

While waiting for his petition to receive proper consideration, Mahomet died from smallpox. He could not be buried in London – it was forbidden for foreigners to be buried in the city – so he was rowed over the water to Southwark and buried in the churchyard of the cathedral in an unmarked grave.

Nearly three centuries later, in 2006, a special stone was brought from America by the Mohegan spiritual leader Bruce 'Two Dogs' Bozsum and fixed in the churchyard in memory of Mahomet. Carved with Mohegan symbols, the stone is designed to appease the dead man's spirit. The queen met Two Dogs at the unveiling and it was as if, at last, the audience that was never given to Mahomet had finally been granted when Two Dogs presented his original petition in person to the queen.

The large, shell-shaped stone can still be seen in Southwark Cathedral churchyard.

ORNATE WATER

⸙

We are so used to having water on tap that it is difficult to recall a time when houses and squares, courtyards and alleyways across London relied on water that had to be pumped by hand from wells dug deep into the London clay.

Until recently it was claimed that at least one of the Inns of Court still privately pumped its water up from the River Fleet, but even if working pumps are now a thing of the past, some wonderful examples remain.

Shoreditch churchyard contains a fine example, as does St Paul's Cathedral, and one or two suburban churchyards now boast pumps moved from their original positions in the streets and kept for sentimental reasons. A fine pump exists by the front wall of St Mary's Church in Acton.

Perhaps the grandest of these memorials to drinking water is the tall, ornate, cast-iron water pump in Bedford Row just off Holborn. Charles Dickens lodged near this and it is easy to imagine he would have helped himself to water here.

But the oddest must be the pump attached to the wall of Staple Inn. The original pump that stood here has long vanished, and the one we see now is a replacement – but it dates to a time long after there was no longer any need for hand pumps and no one seems to have a clue why it was fixed here. It remains one of those unexplained mysteries.

The oldest pump still in its original position is probably the blue painted example at Cornhill just outside the Royal Exchange. This pump is inscribed with the following words: 'On this spot a well was first made and a House of Correction built thereon by Henry Wallis Mayor of London in the year 1282'. The pump is dated 1799.

But perhaps the most interesting specimen of all is the Aldgate Pump, so called because it stands at the junction of Aldgate and Fenchurch Street. It was moved here from Aldgate Pump Court, where a pump had stood from at least the reign of King John. The court was demolished to make way for Fenchurch Street Station but, until 1876, the pump drew its water from an underground stream. It was channelled into the mains system in 1876 after people started to notice that the water had a distinctly chalky flavour. The cause was quickly found: the underground stream ran through a number of plague pits and graveyards on its way to Aldgate and so densely were the skeletons packed in these graveyards that the stream was picking up large amounts of calcium from the bones – enough to impart the distinct taste of chalky bone!

RULE-BREAKING
SCHOOL

❦

Visitors to Westminster Abbey often forget that
a large area around the abbey that is cunningly
hidden by a high, ancient wall is actually a large school.

But this is no ordinary school. Westminster
School (actually 'The Royal College of St Peter in
Westminster') has educated at least seven prime ministers as well as poets John Dryden and Ben Jonson,
author A. A. Milne, architect Sir Christopher Wren
and philosopher Jeremy Bentham.

What makes the school so odd, however, is that, in
addition to exclusively educating the very wealthy, the
school has a dark, murderous past.

In 1679, a group of boys from the school killed a
bailiff, but such was the elite nature of the school that
its headmaster managed to get the boys off scot-free
by paying a fine – the cost of which was then passed
on to all the boys' parents. Ben Jonson also murdered
a man but escaped hanging by pleading his Latin – an
ancient rule that allowed murderers who could read
to escape the noose. They were instead branded with
a hot iron on the thumb – which is what happened
to Jonson.

The school has its own private square and the children are housed in some of central London's most
beautiful and ancient buildings – none of which
can be visited by the general public. Perhaps most

interesting of all is the eighteenth-century mansion hidden inside the school walls. Other ancient buildings here include the fourteenth-century College Hall, eighteenth-century college dormitory and early seventeenth-century Ashburnham House.

The school also has England's oldest continually cultivated garden and its own rifle range. It also has the use of Westminster Abbey as the school chapel.

The school's happy tradition of criminality continued into the twenty-first century when, in 2005, the school was found guilty of the serious offence of running an illegal cartel with other expensive schools to keep its fees as high as possible.

One of the school's maddest customs is known as the Greaze. Each year on Shrove Tuesday, a large pancake reinforced with horsehair (the Greaze) is thrown over an elevated bar, at which point the schoolboys fight for it for exactly one minute. The boy who tears off the biggest piece is traditionally given a golden sovereign (which he immediately gives back).

WOODEN SHOES
CHURCH

∽❧⧉❧∾

Very few London churches escaped the Blitz entirely unscathed. St Katherine Cree in Aldgate, as we have seen, is one such example, but another perhaps less well-known escapee is the curiously named St Margaret Pattens in Eastcheap.

There has been a church on this site since at least the eleventh century. The first was almost certainly a timber building and it was rebuilt in stone some time later. The exact date is not recorded. That church fell into such a state of disrepair that it was demolished in the mid-sixteenth century. Its replacement was destroyed in the Great Fire. The church we see today, designed by Sir Christopher Wren, is remarkable for a number of reasons, not least, of course, the sheer fact of its survival and escape from the Victorian modernisers.

But first that odd name. St Margaret was and still is the guild church of the patten-makers. A patten is a kind of overshoe that has no modern counterpart and disappeared so long ago that many people on hearing the word haven't a clue what it means. Pattens came in many shapes and styles, but were wooden shoes on short stilts. Usually they were slipped on over normal leather shoes rather like a wooden sandal, but the wooden sole was supported by two three-inch wooden pillars. This meant that the wearer could walk

London's filthy, muddy (and often dung-covered) streets while keeping his or her polished leather shoes clean.

At St Margaret's and elsewhere, pattens would have been taken off on Sunday mornings and left at the door.

A curious remnant of St Margaret's connection with the patten-makers can be seen in an old glass case beneath the church tower where numerous examples of pattens dating back to the eighteenth century and earlier have been collected. The case also houses a number of very odd-looking tools that were necessary to carve wooden pattens – the whole structure was made from a single piece of wood to avoid the difficulty of firmly fixing the stilts to the wooden soles. An old sign inside the church still says 'Will the Women remove their pattens before entering the Church'.

But St Margaret's has several other wonderful and rare survivors. The eighteenth-century organ still has its eighteenth-century case (very rare in itself) and there are two canopied churchwardens' pews. These pews with their high doors and covers are unique and remind us that the inside of a church was used to make all sorts of social distinctions in the past. The local aristocrats would often have their own pews where they would be shielded from having to view the great masses of the unwashed.

But perhaps the strangest survivor at St Margaret Pattens is the punishment box, a special pew where sinners were made to sit during services. This rare example even has a devil's head carved on it just to ram the message home!

The outside of the church is very odd too. It includes a 200-foot spire but in a medieval design. No one knows why Wren chose this design given that at the time the church was built most things medieval were seen as crude and barbarous and architects slavishly followed the precepts of classical architecture. The Gothic Revival was still a century and more away and yet in a rare eccentric moment Wren seems to have acknowledged that not all things Gothic were necessarily bad. The spire is also unique as it is the only one of Wren's lead-covered timber spires to survive.

ASPIRING SYDENHAM

The late nineteenth century was a terrible time for London as the hatred of narrow lanes and small courtyards gave way to a craze for broad boulevards and grand imperial buildings. And so it was that the ancient church of St Antholin (originally St Anthony) was taken down in 1875 to make way for Queen Victoria Street.

This beautiful Wren church had been rebuilt after the Great Fire with an especially beautiful spire; in fact this was the only Wren spire built entirely of stone. The church stood opposite Mansion House and the decision to demolish it caused one of the earliest campaigns to preserve an ancient building. Nevertheless, in the face of money and the planners, the church was doomed. It was taken down and dispersed and not a trace remains – or so it was thought, until someone remembered that so loved was the spire that when the church came down a man from Sydenham, then on the very outskirts of south London, bought the stone spire for the princely sum of £5 and, at great further expense, hired a series of large carts to transport it to the garden of his country house.

Round Hill House was a delightful eighteenth-century manor house and Wren's spire became a distinctive feature of the garden. The spire even survived the destruction of Round Hill House itself, so if you want to see a tiny remnant of one of Wren's best churches you can still do so, but unfortunately the spire is now surrounded by a housing estate!

ROMAN REMAINS

❦

There are very few obvious Roman remains in London and in many cases when Roman remains are discovered they are either damaged or hidden or moved. The temple of Mithras famously discovered in Walbrook Street in the 1950s was moved to allow an office block to be built.

Earlier redevelopments were often unsympathetic – but not always.

In medieval London, money and time could be saved by incorporating Roman and medieval work into a new building – which explains why there are far more sections of London's Roman wall surviving than one would at first imagine. The difficulty is that they are often part of the basement walls of nineteenth and early twentieth-century buildings and not open to the public.

But a remarkable and little known Roman survivor – unique in fact in London – is the mosaic floor of a Roman house which was incorporated into the church of All-Hallows-by-the-Tower.

All Hallows is the oldest church in the city but, despite surviving the Great Fire, it was severely damaged by German bombers and only its tower and outer walls survived.

Apart from the mosaic, which is in the Undercroft, the church does have another fascinating survivor from the earliest church on the site – a splendid seventh-century arch that incorporates Roman tile work. The Roman pavement – fine red *tesserae* that looks almost as bright today as it must have looked when first laid here – is largely undamaged.

LOVE LANE HOUSE

❧❦❧

One of the oddest architectural survivors in London can be found near the junction of Love Lane and Wood Street in the City. Here you will find St Alban Tower, which has been converted into flats.

This is the only remaining part of the old Church of St Alban Wood Street. The medieval church that stood here was rebuilt in the 1630s by the great Classical architect Inigo Jones, only to be destroyed in the Great Fire. Wren's replacement church was then destroyed in the Blitz, leaving the tower and the outer walls – the latter demolished in the 1960s. The tower, bizarrely, became a private house and it still is – what's more, it is situated on a traffic island!

A TYPEFACE IN
THE RIVER

A few hundred yards upstream from Hammersmith Bridge along a footpath that looks pretty much today as it did a century and more ago, there is a tiny public house down a narrow alleyway. This is The Dove, an eighteenth-century house whose snug bar, measuring around eight feet by eight feet, is one of the smallest in the country.

The pub was the inspiration for one of London's oddest disputes.

At the beginning of the twentieth century, the bookbinder T. J. Cobden-Sanderson set up the Doves Press just along the river from and named after the Dove public house. His partner was Emery Walker. Cobden-Sanderson was a friend of William Morris and an active supporter of the Arts and Crafts movement.

The press, which inspired many other similar private independent presses, was an attempt to take book making back from the big impersonal printers that had turned bookbinding from a craft into an industrial process.

For eight years, from 1900 to 1908, the two men seem to have got on famously. Walker seems to have been the main designer of the famous Doves Typeface and every single one of the press's books was designed using this typeface and always in the same size.

When the two men fell out, Walker managed to wrest an agreement from his former partner that the rights to the typeface would revert to Walker when Cobden-Sanderson died.

But the legal agreement forgot to mention the physical typefonts themselves. If they were lost or destroyed then the rights to the typeface would be meaningless.

Clearly the spat was a particularly nasty one because Cobden-Sanderson decided early in 1913 to make sure Walker would never get his hands on the typeface. At midnight on 21 March that year, Cobden-Sanderson began throwing all the matrices – the moulds from which the metal type was made – into the River Thames from the middle of Hammersmith Bridge.

A few years later he records in his journals that he began throwing the metal typefonts into the river too – there was so much of it that it took 177 trips!

History does not record Walker's reaction to this – presumably he found out in the end – but all was not lost. In 2015, Robert Green recreated the typeface and then searched the riverbed under Hammersmith Bridge to recover hundreds of pieces of the original type.

Hammersmith Terrace was long the home of William Morris and other Arts and Crafts movement enthusiasts, but especially typographers.

The Doves remains today as a reminder of those heady days more than a century ago, along with the Emery Walker Museum at 7 Hammersmith Terrace, one of London's least-known museums and the last perfect Arts and Crafts interior in existence.

This splendid eighteenth-century house contains

the huge collection of furniture and objects amassed by Walker and preserved by his daughter Dorothy, who died in 1963. The house and its contents survived intact because Dorothy left it to her lifelong companion Elizabeth De Haas who died as recently as 1999, leaving the house and its contents in trust.

SIMPSON'S CHOP HOUSE

❦

The old City's courts and alleyways contained – at least until the Second World War – many early merchant's houses and mansions divided up into small offices or converted into pubs. Better still, many of these alleyways contained what was once a city institution – the chop house. This was a cheap restaurant where city workers could eat their lunch. Most were characterised by a room divided by wood panels into small snug areas where friends could meet undisturbed.

Most of the courts and alleyways, the mansions and chop houses were swept away by bombs and redevelopment; those courts that remained became sanitised with bright new bars and tall office blocks replacing the old subdivided houses, but against all the odds at least one chop house has survived in its original court.

Simpson's can be found in Ball Court right in the heart of the old City. It still has a vaguely eighteenth-century appearance because it was founded in 1757 and still has its panelled, divided snuggeries.

ON YOUR MARKS

Bevis Marks Synagogue is reasonably well known. It was completed in 1701 and has suffered only minor damage and alteration in the intervening years. Based on the great synagogue of Amsterdam, which was completed in the early 1670s, Bevis Marks is remarkable for being the only synagogue in Europe to have offered services continuously for more than 300 years. Synagogues across Europe were frequently burned to the ground in regular uprisings against Jews and even the great Amsterdam synagogue lost much of its interior after it was closed by the Nazis – the galleries were removed and used as firewood, for example.

But Bevis Marks soldiered on unscathed.

Perhaps its most unusual feature is the massive ark in which the Torah scrolls are kept. Even on close inspection this looks like yellow marble, yet it is not – in fact, it is cunningly painted solid oak.

Bevis Marks is also odd in that most city churches are free to enter if they are open, but Bevis Marks charges an entrance fee and usually has a fearsome-looking bouncer lurking at the door. Curiously unwelcoming.

TURKISH DELIGHT

～〰✦〰～

Travellers enjoying the Grand Tour during the eighteenth and nineteenth centuries returned to England and brought with them a taste for Turkish baths. These were enjoyed not just in Turkey, to which the classically educated English gentleman would not usually have travelled, but they were also a feature of Greece, which was then under Ottoman rule and a popular part of any aristocratic cultural tour.

By the mid-nineteenth century, Turkish baths were all the rage and magnificent examples were built in Jermyn Street, Northumberland Avenue and elsewhere in the city. They were often built in a Moorish style – with elaborate tiled walls, glittering mosaics and tinkling fountains.

In the heart of the city there were several Turkish baths and for a long time it was assumed none had survived. Then, in the early 1970s, Nevill's Turkish Baths in New Broad Street were rediscovered. The building had ceased to function as a Turkish bath in the early 1950s when Turkish baths in general went out of fashion and for many years it was used as a storeroom, its marvellous interior gradually fading under decades of dust and dirt.

There had been a bath of some sort in New Broad Street as early as 1817. The Argyll Medical Baths were established here in 1847, but, as the name implies, the idea was to offer baths as a cure for various ailments rather than as a pleasurable experience. The addition of Turkish baths in 1860 was a recognition that baths could be had simply for the pleasure of a good scrub.

Jones and Co. took over the baths in the 1880s, only to sell them on to James and Henry Forder Nevill in 1889.

By 1895, the baths we see today had been built and they were and are the last word in Moorish decadence.

After entering a small space at street level, the bather descended a winding staircase lined with gleaming colourful tiles to a small room in the basement where he bought his ticket. He then entered a cooling room where he could lie on a divan in a small cubicle, listen to a fountain playing and enjoy the Alhambra style of the decorative scheme. Beyond the cooling room were three increasingly warm rooms, all magnificently decorated with coloured tiles.

The staircase was of oak, the panels of walnut – this was a place of conspicuous luxury.

So successful was the enterprise that, in 1908, the Nevills sold shares in the company. By this time they had baths at Whitechapel, London Bridge, Commercial Road and the Wool Exchange.

So if you want to see one of the City's great survivors and eat where once London's wealthy lounged in Eastern luxury you can. Even if you don't go in, you can enjoy the visual extravaganza of the little Moorish kiosk with its tiles and arches and dome – all above ground and free for all to see.

MEDIEVAL CONDUIT

Medieval London drew its water from the Thames, but as the river became dirtier people began to complain that their ale (beer was a later invention relying on imported German hops) began to taste unpleasant. A decision was made to bring water to the city via conduits (stone and brick channels underground) that tapped into streams and underground springs on the northern hills of Hampstead and Highgate.

Lamb's Conduit Street in Holborn recalls a water supply repaired in 1564 by Sir William Lamb.

The Holborn conduit supplied water from a dam created in the upper reaches of the old Fleet River. You can still see what's left of the old Lamb's Conduit Head – the remnants were incorporated into the wall of a 1950s building at the corner of Long Yard and Lamb's Conduit Street.

An even more ancient conduit was the Great Conduit that ran from Tyburn – modern Marble Arch – through wooden pipes all the way to the city. The route it took was across fields to Charing Cross then along the Strand and Fleet Street and thence to the City. The Great Conduit was built in the 1240s and the miles of conduit eventually reached a small stone building where citizens would take their buckets to fill. Nothing of the Great Conduit remains (it ceased to be used after the Great Fire), although occasionally when work is being carried out along its old route stretches of wooden pipe are discovered. If you want to see the best preserved conduit head in London, however, you'll need to go to Myddelton Passage in Islington.

Here you will find the fourteenth-century 'Chimney' or 'Devil's Conduit', which stood in Queen Square, Bloomsbury until about 1912. The origins of its name are mysterious, but a remarkable photograph taken in 1912 shows the water still streaming along a channel down a stone slope inside the conduit and heading towards the City, which it had supplied for more than 600 years. Unfortunately this fascinating piece of history fell victim to the developers and it was destroyed, but at least the building that had allowed access to the stream at this point was preserved. It was taken to Islington in 1927 and rebuilt, and today it can be seen behind an office building.

It is made of Portland stone and has a flat stone roof and upper and lower chambers. The stone construction – rather than cheaper timber or brick – shows how important piped water was to the city more than five centuries ago.

The Chimney Conduit is said to have been an extension of the even more ancient White Conduit, which once brought water to Greyfriars monastery, later Christ's Hospital on Newgate Street.

FROM PANORAMA
TO CHURCH

❧❦❧

J ust north of Leicester Square in Leicester Place is
a curious church that most people hardly glance
at twice. Certainly from the outside the building is
not especially noteworthy, though it is a survivor from
the 1860s when the French Marist fathers bought the
old Burford's Panorama that had been here for more
than half a century. The Marists (actually 'the Society
of Mary') were founded in the nineteenth century
and given responsibility for bringing Christianity to
Africa and elsewhere.

The panorama they bought in London was an early
form of cinema that showed a painted scene that was
slowly turned by a system of wheels and cogs so that
spectators gathered in the centre of the panorama
were given the impression that they were watching a
great procession.

But the Marists needed a place for the French
community in London to worship and so they re-
constructed the panorama to create a church that still
offers services to this day. But what is little known
is that the round church follows the exact shape of
the panorama and may even incorporate parts of the
earlier structure. The architect of the new church,
the largely forgotten Louis-Auguste Boileau, used a
revolutionary material for his new church – cast iron.

The Church of Notre Dame de France is also

remarkable for its extraordinary murals by Jean Cocteau (1889–1963). Cocteau is best known as a film maker, but towards the end of his life he came to London especially to paint the murals in this church. The pictures have a vaguely Post-Impressionist air and show scenes from the life of Christ, as well as a self-portrait of Cocteau. There is also a splendid mosaic by the Russian artist Boris Anrep (1883–1969) who was a close friend of the Bloomsbury Group and completed a better known mosaic at the nearby National Gallery using his Bloomsbury friends as models.

POET'S STOLEN
FURNITURE

❧❦❧

Consecrated in 1817, St Marylebone Parish Church – its portico based on the Pantheon in Rome – replaced a small brick church built in 1740. The old church became a chapel at ease and survived until 1949 when it was demolished.

But what makes St Marylebone Church so interesting is that it was here that one of the greatest love affairs of the nineteenth century reached its celebrated conclusion.

The story of Robert Browning's elopement with Elizabeth Barrett is too well known to repeat at length, but the essence of the story is that the great poet fell in love with a girl who appears to have spent much of her life before meeting Browning resting on a sofa in the way that delicate, middle-class women were supposed to at that time.

Her father by all accounts made great efforts to convince his daughter that she was too ill for any of the usual pleasures of life, let alone marriage, but when she and Browning met they fell in love and, knowing how opposed her father would be to the match, the two married in secret – at St Marylebone Church – and eloped to Italy. The story became one of the great love stories of the Victorian era and for many years the church preserved much of Browning's furniture in a room kept apart for the purpose.

Today all that remains is the church register recording their marriage, however, for the furniture has all, bit by bit, been stolen.

The room, bare and functional today, is now used for meetings.

NEWGATE CELLS

❧❦❧

The Viaduct Tavern at Holborn is a glorious piece of Victorian architecture, but according to some historians it has a dark secret.

If you ask nicely, you may be shown the cellars, which it is claimed are actually part of the cells of the old Newgate Prison. Certainly the pub is roughly in the right place and the cellars do have a prison-like feel to them, so the story may well be true – especially as builders at one time tended to use cellars and foundations already in place when they built their new buildings because it was cheaper than digging out new foundations and had no effect on the appearance of the outside of the new building.

The only other place you can see a section of Newgate is at the end of Amen Corner near St Paul's, where a stretch of high wall survives.

BURIED AT
SOMERSET HOUSE

S omerset House – built at the end of the eighteenth
century – may not be as interesting at the Tudor
palace it replaced, but it does have some intriguing
aspects.

This vast palace was built as a statement – there had
long been complaints that London did not have a huge
official building created in the most up-to-date architectural style. The new Somerset House was meant to
remedy this, with its long Neoclassical Strand frontage and even more impressive river frontage.

Until the Embankment was built, the Thames
flowed under the walls of Somerset House and the
river terrace, painted by Canaletto among others, was
one of the sights of London.

But less well known is the curiously named
Somerset Deadhouse. This is a long passageway that
allows daylight to reach the windows of the basement
rooms of the palace. The narrow passageway is hugely
popular with makers of period films – most recently
Sherlock Holmes starring Robert Downey Jr.

But here and there along these passageways are
tombstones. They are believed to date from the time
of the earlier palace and almost certainly from the
chapel built by Charles II for his French (and therefore Catholic) wife Queen Henrietta Maria. The
chapel and its burial ground were demolished along

with the whole Tudor palace, but some of the tomb-stones were repositioned discreetly here in the new palace, presumably at the express request of someone in the royal family with Catholic sympathies. Placing the tombs in the Deadhouse would have been discreet enough to avoid arousing the anger of the London population, which by the end of the eighteenth century was going through a fiercely anti-Catholic phase.

SICK IN PICTURES

Most people have come across prints of Hogarth's work, but the great artist's eccentricities are less well known. His house at Chiswick escaped demolition and it is now bordered by the noisy A4 road, but the interior and garden are much as Hogarth would have known. Especially eccentric is a wonderful device he created that allowed him to open his bedroom door to his servant without getting out of bed – it's a bell pull by the bed head attached to a pulley that runs across the ceiling and down to the bolt on the door.

Hogarth's tomb also survives in the nearby churchyard, but sadly the church he knew was rebuilt (apart from the tower) in the 1800s. In his lifetime, and for long afterwards, he was such a popular artist that his pictures were widely engraved and disseminated via prints.

Hogarth was a great patriot and when he heard that an Italian artist had been asked to paint the walls of the staircase of the great hall at St Bartholomew's Hospital, he was so incensed he offered to do the work himself for nothing. Understandably the authorities jumped at this opportunity to procure the work of the greatest artist of the day at no cost.

Hogarth painted two main scenes – the Pool of Bethesda and the Good Samaritan.

Most people think the pictures are murals and printed directly on to plaster but, in fact, they are painted on canvas and attached to the walls.

The Pool of Bethesda was painted in the artist's studio in St Martin's Lane near the present church of St Martin-in-the-Fields, but the Good Samaritan was painted from scaffolding specially erected for the artist in the hall itself.

Both large-scale pictures were finished and in position by 1737 and are one of London's greatest artistic secrets.

The choice of the Pool of Bethesda comes from the Bible story where the pool is known for its healing properties.

The significance of the Good Samaritan painting needs no explanation, but what's curious about the Pool of Bethesda picture is that many if not most of the models for the figures were patients at the hospital – one figure appears to have rickets, then a common complaint, another is blind, yet another arthritic, another suffers from jaundice. It has even been suggested that one of the figures is suffering from a depressive disorder. Until recently part of every medical student's training included viewing these pictures as the signs of the various illnesses depicted are so accurate.

Hogarth was very proud of these pictures and insisted on returning in the years after they were painted to personally clean them. He also insisted that they should never be varnished – his wishes were ignored and by the early twentieth century when they were cleaned they may have had as many as a dozen layers of varnish on them.

Hogarth was born in St Bartholomew Lane, so he felt a special interest in this work. He certainly spent a great deal of time and effort ensuring these are among his masterworks – despite not being paid a penny.

CATFORD PREFABS

After the Second World War there was a feeling in Britain that we could not go back to the old pre-war world where the poor simply had to put up with damp, unheated houses and depressed wages.

The feeling stemmed from the fact that the working classes had provided most of the soldiers who fought to defeat the Nazis. So they deserved better, especially as so many of the upper classes had quietly sent their sons to Ireland and elsewhere to avoid them having to be called up.

But, of course, there was a major problem – so many houses had been destroyed by German bombers, especially in London, that it wasn't a question of better housing so much as a question of any housing at all.

Such was the shortage of housing that the government came up with the idea of building prefabs – prefabricated houses that would be quick and cheap to build. Put together in a few days from factory-made panels, prefabs sprang up all over the country and with their small gardens and neat, cosy appearance, they were a huge success.

But, as they were meant to last only a decade or so, almost all have now been demolished. But there is one place, where you can still see these remarkable little houses – Catford in south-east London. Here the last big estate of prefabs survived, incredibly, until 2014.

What makes the Excalibur Estate unusual and

interesting is that the panels and chimneys, the floors, ceilings and other components of these houses were delivered by lorries driven by German and Italian prisoners of war who then helped put the pieces together.

Though the Excalibur Estate has been demolished, six prefabs have been saved by English Heritage and now form a new museum where you can see a typical prefab, its interior decorated just as it would have been in the 1940s and 1950s.

GRUESOME RELICS

❧⊱◈⊰❧

The outskirts of London were once dotted with convents and monasteries. Many sprang up during the nineteenth century after John Henry Newman converted to Rome and made Catholicism respectable and even fashionable.

This was an extraordinary transformation for, in the eighteenth century, Catholics were still occasionally persecuted and they were banned from many professions. Of course, this didn't stop aristocratic families such as the Dukes of Norfolk retaining the old religion, but for ordinary Catholics life could be difficult. Then a gradual liberalisation of society combined with a passion for Gothic art and architecture gradually made Catholicism seem more solidly English than Anglicanism, which had, after all, been established to a large extent by Henry VIII, a most unattractive man whose main hobby appears to have been collecting wives.

Once Catholicism was back in fashion, Westminster Cathedral was built, along with hundreds of other new Catholic churches up and down the country.

Close to Marble Arch in Hyde Park Place a small Catholic convent was established and, remarkably, despite the closure of so many of these suburban convents, this one still survives.

What makes the Tyburn Convent especially interesting is that the nuns set up their convent here to be near the place where so many Catholics had been killed for their faith. The nuns live a largely silent life, for this is a strict order – officially known as The Benedictine Adorers of the Sacred Heart of Jesus of Montmartre, founded in 1898. The convent has twelve sister houses around the world and the order follows the rule of St Benedict. Nuns wear traditional habits and though not strictly silent there are long periods of silence every day.

This curious medieval survival in west London is made stranger still by the relics the convent contains. Above the altar in the chapel is a gruesome reminder of the past: a reproduction of the Tyburn gallows where more than 100 Catholic martyrs were killed. The Catholic passion for relics can be seen here in all its glory: the convent's collection includes a small piece of linen and some straw stained with the blood of five Catholics killed at Tyburn in the seventeenth century; there is a finger from John Roberts who was hanged, drawn and quartered at Tyburn in 1610; a lock of hair from an unidentified martyr; and, perhaps most gruesome of all, a fingernail from the Jesuit Thomas Holland who died at Tyburn in December 1642.

RIVER POLICE MUSEUM

England has a reputation for eccentricity and, among a host of eccentric institutions, top of the list must be our museums. There are fan museums, lawnmower museums and even fishing-reel museums, but in London you would have to go a long way to find a more eccentric museum than the River Police Museum at Wapping Police Station.

This splendid building is still a working police station but in the old carpenter's workshop you will find a unique collection of old uniforms, truncheons and even cutlasses – cutlasses (a sort of curved sword) were issued to the river police for some years after they were founded in 1798.

The river police were set up in response to the enormous amount of contraband that came up the river and the fact that it was easy for criminals to escape by boat to the southern shore if they were pursued by a bobby. The smugglers' trick was to leave a boat tied up at the bottom of one of the numerous flights of stairs that led down to the water, much as a criminal might have a getaway car today.

For the first century and more after they were established, the river police rowed themselves up and down the river and, since they were not always as hardy as the criminal rowers, it was not always easy to make arrests. Around 1900 they finally acquired a paraffin-engined boat and from there eventually the diesel-powered launches of today.

RAGGED SCHOOL

Anyone who knows London will have noticed those distinctive tall, red-brick, vaguely Gothic schools known originally as board schools. They were mostly built between 1880 and 1910 in a very similar and rather grand style as the very first attempt at mass education for the poor. At first, it is true, some of them charged six pence a week, but soon even that charge was dropped and millions of poor Londoners began at last to be educated. Before the establishment of these schools, only the middle and upper classes who could pay – and it was expensive – were able to send their children to school and then often only until the age of twelve. Secondary education was solely for the elite, so London was home to millions of illiterate or semi-literate people who were often too poor even to know how to make the best of what little they had.

Before these board schools were set up by the government, however, there was a valiant attempt by a number of private charities to provide education for the poor.

The ragged schools – or 'free schools' as they were known at the time – were the brainchild of Dubliner Thomas Barnardo. He had come to London intending to train as a doctor and missionary but was so appalled by the state in which the poor lived in London that he decided to do something about it. He opened a number of free schools including, in 1877, the Copperfield Road Free School. For thirty years this provided thousands of poor East End children with a free education. It closed in 1908 for the simple reason that the government had taken Barnardo's hint and set up enough government board schools to make Copperfield Road redundant.

The school had been based in a series of old warehouses by the side of the Regent's Canal and after it closed the warehouses were abandoned. Faced with demolition in the 1980s, they were saved by a group of local people who wanted to open a museum to remind the world how free education in London had really begun.

As luck would have it, the buildings had never been modernised; they have been kitted out with desks and blackboards once again and as a result they look just as they would have looked a century and a half ago.

SPIKY BRIDGE

The current London Bridge is the third to cross the river at this point on the Thames and it is also the least interesting. Gone are the towers and turrets of earlier structures; the picturesque houses and privies overhanging the water.

But the bridge's most gruesome feature had always been the long wooden spikes that stood high above the towers built at the southern end. It was on these spikes that for centuries traitors' heads were impaled.

When the old bridge was demolished, the new Georgian bridge was built slightly upstream of the old bridge (in the process destroying the seventeenth-century Fishmonger's Hall) but all traces of those old barbarous spikes were removed.

When the Georgian bridge was sold in the 1960s and shipped stone by stone to the United States, a new purely functional bridge was built to replace it. This is the bridge we now have, but its builders did add one feature that serves as a reminder of the ancient uses to which this river crossing was once put. If you look carefully at the southern end of the bridge you will see a large spike – it's a modern version of those medieval traitors' head spikes. Let us hope this one remains unused!

GARRICK UNDER
THE ROAD

Shakespeare was famously bowdlerised in the
eighteenth century to try to make his gruesome
endings more positive and his profanities less shocking. Thus *King Lear* was given a happy ending, with
Cordelia surviving to live happily ever after. The word
bowdlerise comes from the writer Thomas Bowdler
(1754–1825) who wanted to make Shakespeare more
decorous so that he could be read aloud to a family
without the risk of impropriety. But, despite this sense
that Shakespeare was rude and vulgar, he was revered
in the eighteenth century in particular, and nowhere
more so than in the mind of the great actor David
Garrick (1717–79), of whom his friend Dr Johnson
said 'The theatre made Garrick rich and he made the
theatre respectable.'

Garrick was so obsessed by Shakespeare that in 1756
he built a temple to the great playwright at Hampton,
west of London on the Thames and close to the former
home of the great Augustan poet Alexander Pope.
After a recent restoration, this remarkable building is
now open to the public, but only on Sundays.

The temple looks rather like a small version of
the Pantheon at Rome – it is a single room with a
dome and a four-column Ionic entrance that faces
east. Garrick built it to house his collection of
Shakespearian artefacts.

A chair made for Garrick by Hogarth from a mulberry tree said to have grown in the garden of Shakespeare's house in Stratford was sold after Garrick's death and is now in the Folger Shakespeare Library in Washington, while a statue of Shakespeare by Louis-François Roubiliac (who used Garrick as a model) is now in the British Museum.

But what is really so intriguing about this temple by the Thames is that, to make sure he could get to it easily each day from his house nearby, Garrick had to dig a tunnel under a roadway. He used to learn his lines by walking up and down the tunnel where nothing could distract him – 'not even birdsong', as he put it – and the temple was kept for 'contemplation' and as a place where Garrick could write to his huge number of friends. Indeed, Garrick was such a prolific writer that the postman would call especially each day to collect a sack of letters.

BLOCKHEADS

London clubs are one of the city's more embar-rassing features. Some refuse to have women members; most don't allow visitors. The very grand clubs – White's, Boodles and so on – don't even iden-tify themselves by having a name plaque on the front door, presumably to avoid the risk of common people wandering in.

The old joke that half the old buffers sitting in the drawing rooms of these clubs are actually dead, how-ever, has more than a grain of truth, because the stuffi-est of these clubs are the last bastion of the old buffer.

But the oldest of the clubs have done at least one great service – they have preserved one or two splen-did buildings that would almost certainly have been demolished without them. And a very curious tale surrounds the fate of one of the less lucky of these clubs – the Junior Carlton.

The Junior Carlton was set up in response to the Second Reform Act of 1867, which created a whole new set of electors. It was called the Junior Carlton because prospective members – though Tory to a man – knew they had no hope of being admitted to the Carlton Club itself. They were not from old families and had only recently made their money, so they were not quite acceptable to the members of the older club. Membership of the Carlton proper was reserved for far grander figures of the establishment.

The Junior Carlton's clubhouse, a large and rather splendid nineteenth-century building, was at 30 Pall Mall. All went well until 1963, when the people who ran the club decided to sell their building in order to buy the land next to it. The land they had their eye on had formerly been occupied by the Carlton Club, but the building on the site had been destroyed by a bomb in the Second World War.

The plan went ahead and the committee that ran the Junior Carlton bought the plot and decided to build what they described as 'the club of the future'. This was a concrete and steel-and-glass box. Within months of the new building opening the members were cancelling their subscriptions in droves. In 1977 the club merged with the Carlton Club as virtually all its members had left.

MAGGS'S GHOST

❧

L ondon is full of ghosts. Most theatres more than a
century old are said to have ghosts – usually bad-
tempered actors who did not succeed in their careers
– and many churches are the same, their ghosts usually women who died of a broken heart or disgruntled
vicars with a grudge against their former parishioners.

But it is very rare for an ordinary shop to have a
well-attested ghost, which is why Maggs Bros Ltd,
the antiquarian bookseller's in Mayfair, is so unusual.

Maggs is one of the oldest and most prestigious
antiquarian booksellers in the world. Their shop, in a
beautiful Georgian building in Berkeley Square, at-
tracts collectors from all over the world and at Maggs
it would not be difficult to spend £100,000 on a single
book. They will sell you an individual book but they
much prefer, as they say themselves, to build relationships with collectors who buy regularly. This means
the shop can be rather intimidating if you are not
already a millionaire bibliophile.

No. 50 Berkeley Square has been Maggs's home
since the middle of the twentieth century, but in the
nineteenth century this house was known as the most
haunted in London. So much so that for many years
it remained empty as no tenant could be found to take
on the lease.

In his 1907 book *Haunted Houses*, Charles Harper
records that, during a period when the house was

untenanted in the 1850s, lights were often seen flashing in the upstairs windows and faint screams could be heard by passers-by. The whole west side of Berkeley Square came to be avoided by the superstitious who preferred to cross by the east side and avoid the risk of hearing unearthly groans.

The legend of this haunted house seems to stem from an early tenant, who kept his mad and extremely violent brother locked in the attic, feeding him twice a day through a hatch in the door.

Visitors to Maggs as recently as 2005 reported occasionally seeing odd shadows flitting through the building or sensing a presence. One visitor even had his glasses knocked off as he walked up the stairs. Understandably in its literature and advertisement Maggs make no mention of these strange goings-on...

LIFE IN THE
CHURCH TOWER

War-damaged churches were often rebuilt and great efforts, in some cases, were made to replicate the internal features that had been destroyed. St James's Church in Piccadilly is a good example. Other churches were left in their damaged state or their towers were kept while the rest of the church was demolished.

Christ Church Greyfriars, which was also sometimes known as Christ Church Newgate Street, is a case in point. Greyfriars refers to the clothing of the Franciscan monks who lived in the attached priory, but worshipped here. The priory buildings were also home to Christ's School, a foundation that survives but long ago moved out of London.

By the early 1930s, the congregation at Christ Church Greyfriars had declined to a few dozen and then, on 29 December 1940, a firebomb destroyed the church including all its fittings – with one extraordinary exception. For reasons even he could not later explain, a passing fireman ran into the burning church and rescued the beautifully carved, late-seventeenth-century wooden font cover.

He said afterwards that he felt a strange compulsion to run into the church, despite the danger, and though he had never previously been inside and knew nothing of the contents, he felt the font cover had to be saved.

Perhaps the strangest thing about this church, however, is that the tower, which survived the fire, was taken apart stone by stone after the war ended and then reassembled in exactly the same place. The idea was to strengthen it with modern building materials including steel beams.

Inevitably, as this was the 1960s, part of the old churchyard – which had been the site of the medieval monastery – was taken for street widening and then in 1981 an office block (equally inevitably) was built in the south-west corner of the old churchyard.

The rebuilt tower was converted into several flats which are inhabited to this day. So, if you want to live in a Wren-designed tower in central London, keep an eye on local estate agents...

THE LAST
OSTLER'S HOUSE

❧⟨⟩❧

The role of the ostler is one that vanished with the coming of the motor car. Before motorised transport, thousands of men up and down the country spent their lives in this ancient profession. Their job was to attend to their master's horses. That meant that when a gentleman returned to his house on horseback (or in his carriage), it was the ostler's job to take his horse to the stable, feed it and settle it for the night.

Ostlers were also employed by the thousands of inns across the country that existed to serve the needs of travellers and their horses.

London still has one remnant of this ancient trade and it is overlooked by almost everyone – the ostler's hut in Lincoln's Inn Fields.

This is said to be the smallest listed building in London. It is certainly one of the most charming. It has a vaguely Gothic appearance – red brick, with stone detailing. For more than forty years after it was built in 1860, the hut was where the ostler attached to Lincoln's Inn looked after the horses of the lawyers and their visitors. The hut fell out of use early in the twentieth century and was quietly forgotten as horses gradually disappeared from London's streets.

BILLY'S PALACE
IN THE MALL

William Tallon was one of the most extraordinary characters of the twentieth century. For fifty-two years he was the most trusted servant of the late Queen Mother. The son of a shopkeeper from the Midlands, Tallon was in fact far more than a servant – the Queen Mother took him everywhere with her and their relationship caused huge problems in the royal household because the Queen Mother made it very clear that even her aristocratic advisers were of less value to her than Tallon. She once famously said to an adviser who disliked Billy: 'Your job is negotiable. Billy's is not.'

It was this attitude that led many people to think of Billy and the Queen Mother almost as one would think of a couple.

He may have been a servant – his official title was Groom of the Backstairs – but most observers thought he was far more like the Queen Mother's life partner. They dressed up in fancy dress together, went out for private lunches, attended the opera together and partied late into the night. Tallon was a key element in the organisation of the Queen Mother's favourite daily event – lunch. He made her guests drink and helped them relax so that they could entertain the Queen Mother.

Most servants were given a small bed-sitting room

at the top of one or other of the royal London palaces, but, after a time, Tallon was given a little house of his own. This strange little house – which he called 'my little palace in the Mall' – became the scene of constant riotous parties where Tallon would entertain his many friends with champagne and endless jokes and anecdotes. His only stipulation was that his guests should leave quietly as the Queen Mother – whose bedroom was just a few hundred feet away – slept with her bedroom window open.

Tallon stayed in his 'little palace' until the Queen Mother's death in 2002. From the outside, the house is unchanged since Tallon's time – he died in 2007 – and it can still be seen, rather like a low-built Georgian bungalow, halfway along the Mall toward Admiralty Arch from Buckingham Palace.

A TOWER IN
KENSINGTON

One of the oddest architectural survivors in London
can be found in South Kensington. Here, the
whole area south of the Albert Memorial was designed by Victorian planners as a huge centre for the
arts and sciences. This is why you find the Victoria
and Albert Museum, the Science Museum and the
Natural History Museum all together and within a
street or two of each other. The Royal College of Art
is also based here and the Royal Geographical Society
has its delightful red-brick headquarters opposite
Hyde Park at the top of the appropriately named
Exhibition Road. Just along from here is the magnificent Royal Albert Hall, the Victorians' vast circular
homage to music.

The modern buildings of Imperial College seem
incongruous when viewed against the magnificence
of these Victorian buildings, yet they are wedged between the Albert Hall and the Science Museum.

How on earth did they get here?

The answer is that they are only here because, in
addition to the existing temples to the various arts and
sciences that survive, there was once another building here – the Imperial Institute. Completed in 1894,
the Imperial Institute was a huge, part-Gothic, part-
Renaissance-style building very much in the style of
the V&A and the Natural History Museum nearby,

but if anything it was even more ornate. It was built to promote research that could benefit the empire, but in reality this meant finding ways to develop science and industry in countries around the world that were ruled by Britain.

Perhaps because the empire was rapidly diminishing, a decision was taken to demolish the Imperial Institute. The building, in all its magnificence, was condemned and gradually demolished and the Imperial Institute morphed into the Commonwealth Institute based in the old gardens of Holland House at the other end of Kensington High Street.

On the former site of the old Imperial Institute the new buildings of Imperial College that we see today were built. Rather like a gigantic public lavatory, they now surround the one part of the old Imperial Institute that was preserved – the huge ornate tower. The Queen's Tower as it is known is a staggering 87 metres tall and one of London's lesser known architectural gems.

BEATING THE RIVER

All Hallows by the Tower is London's oldest church, although much that we see today represents post-war rebuilding. The church, which was probably founded in the seventh century, is also the starting place for one of the city's most unusual ceremonies, known as 'beating the bounds'.

English villages across the country still beat the bounds each spring and wherever you go, from Lincolnshire to Cornwall, from Herefordshire to Kent, you will find parishes that still take part in this old custom. The point of it is to reassert and confirm all the land that comes within a particular parish. This was far more important in previous times than it is now because maps were rudimentary and often inaccurate. Also, on the basis that good fences make good neighbours, it was always a good idea to remind people every year exactly who owned what and where.

Beating the bounds at All Hallows may well date back to the time when this was still a rural area. Generally speaking, beating the bounds ceremonies normally took place on Rogation days (days of fasting) but at All Hallows the ceremony takes place on Ascension Day.

Masters of various livery companies take part as well as the clergy, and at various points around the parish the ground is beaten with canes. Most eccentric of all is the process of beating the parish's southern boundary – because this just happens to be halfway across the Thames! Undaunted, the All Hallows team hire a boat and move out until they are mid-stream. Canes are then used to give the river a good thrashing and make sure the middle of the river really knows where it is!

A similar ceremony was formerly carried out by officials from the Fishmongers' Company. In medieval times they ritually beat the waters of the Thames to remind the fish that they were essential to life in London.

The practice ended when London's river became so polluted that all fishing ceased and the fishmongers had to get their catch from further downstream and out to sea.

FOUNDLING'S ACORN

❧✦❧

O nly the gatehouses survive of one of London's most remarkable eighteenth-century institutions – the Foundling Hospital set up by Thomas Coram in 1739. Coram was horrified at the way children and babies were allowed to die in the streets of London. He spent nearly twenty years petitioning the government to do something about it and at last a Royal Charter allowed the creation of the hospital, effectively the world's first orphanage, in open fields in Bloomsbury.

Babies could be left anonymously in a specially designed alcove in one of the outer walls and every child was taken in. The Foundling Hospital survived on its Bloomsbury site until the 1920s when most of the buildings were demolished and the charity moved to Redhill in Surrey where it continues to this day.

You can still visit the Coram fields and see the gatehouses and part of the outer wall; the grounds where the old buildings once stood are kept as a children's play area.

The Coram Museum in Redhill boasts a number of curious exhibits, including some of the pitiful items destitute mothers left with their babies when they were forced to abandon them. These items include a penny, a silver chain and even – perhaps saddest of all – an acorn.

Remarkably, the Foundling Hospital still has the records of more than 25,000 children who passed through its doors.

WORLD'S LONGEST ROPE

Camden Market in north London is one of the most popular shopping destinations in the capital. Packed with stalls selling clothing – everything from the bizarre to the retro – the market is especially popular as many of its buildings were once associated with horses and barge traffic on the canal that runs through the site.

Indeed, the whole of the market area has a wonderful historic feel to it. It is rambling and ramshackle, rather like a medieval souk, and many of the stalls have been set up in the old stables where the bargees' horses were once housed.

Beneath Camden Market, things are even more exciting, for here there are miles of underground caverns and storerooms. Indeed, they stretch for such a distance that it has never been considered safe to open them to the public.

There is also a large subterranean hall, constructed in 1837 for the London and Birmingham Railway – a truly remarkable survivor.

It once housed a huge steam engine and cable-winding mechanism designed to haul steam trains up the hill from Euston Station in the days when the steep incline (1 in 85) was too much for the engines then in use. Despite the skill of the great engineer Isambard Kingdom Brunel who built the railway here, nothing could be done to reduce the steepness of the climb north out of the station. The ingenious solution was this remarkable winding engine.

The stairs down to the wheelhouse still exist and the wheelhouse itself is thirty-five metres long, seven metres high and four-and-a-half metres wide – all constructed of magnificent brickwork and shaped stone. An operator waited for a signal from Euston Station a mile or so down the hill; he would set the coal-driven steam engine going and the train would be hauled up the hill at around fifteen miles an hour until the incline was sufficiently gentle to allow the carriages to be coupled to a locomotive that would continue the journey under its own steam.

The rope used was the longest piece of unspliced rope ever created, at almost 4,000 yards long. It was seven inches in circumference and weighed more than eleven tons!

Double engines (two locomotives coupled together at the front of the carriages) were used from 1847 to pull trains up the hill and the winding house fell into disuse, its machinery demolished. But the fact that the hall was so long forgotten helped its survival and, thankfully, it is now a listed struture.

NANNIES IN THE DELL

There is a delightful corner of Hyde Park that, while hardly anyone notices it today, until the Second World War had the highest social cachet of anywhere in the park.

On any day in spring or summer the casual observer would have seen smartly dressed women with very large prams heading towards this corner of the park from the mansions of Mayfair and Belgravia. These women were not the mothers of the infants in their prams; these were full-time, professional nannies employed by aristocratic women to take care of their children while they socialised and tried to do as little as possible. To have some form of employment meant that one was not out of the top drawer; real aristocrats were proud of the fact that they did nothing at all and one result of this of course was that nannies had to be employed, generation after generation, to look after any children.

But the nannies who gathered in this corner of Hyde Park were no ordinary nannies. Rather like an army, they wore severe starched uniforms, heavy wool coats (even in summer) and absurd badges on their caps. They all dressed identically because their uniforms were supplied by the same aristocratic organisation – the Norland Agency. They all pushed huge, expensive, Silver Cross prams – like miniature sprung carriages – and on each the crest of the relevant family would be prominently displayed. Such was the absurd snobbery associated with all this that only middle-class girls were accepted for Norland nanny training, part of which included elocution lessons and learning how to speak with unimaginably clipped vowels.

Part of their regular daily duties included wheeling their charges to Hyde Park or Kensington Gardens. Even here, however, there were special rules, because not just anywhere in the park would do.

When they reached the park the nannies and their charges were allowed through a set of gates into what was and is still known as the Dell. Here a beautifully kept lawn swept down through mature trees and shrubs to a tiny stream – a remnant of the old Westbourne River that was dug out in the eighteenth century to form the Serpentine.

At the Knightsbridge end of the Serpentine, a culvert allows water to overflow under a bridge and down a short waterfall into the stream that runs next to the Dell before disappearing underground until it reaches the Thames near Chelsea Bridge.

Only those (in the correct clothing) with huge gleaming prams and aristocratic employers were allowed into the Dell. Lesser mortals with less grand employers, even if wealthy, were not allowed to sit in that idyllic spot. Once in the Dell, the nannies – famously dragon-like according to the writer Eric Newby – would allow their charges to sit on the grass if it was very fine and to mix exclusively with babies from their own set.

The absurdity of all this was destroyed by the Second World War which somehow made it less admirable to do nothing; allowing the already privileged to have even more privileges suddenly became rather absurd. Today the Dell can be seen from the path that runs nearby, but it is closed to the public and the beautiful lawns and mature trees play host only to songbirds and the ghosts of those long-dead aristocratic children.

MISTRESS OF
THE STREETS

The royal family has always existed, in part at least, so that the rest of us have something to look up to; the family came to represent, as it were, a moral exemplar for ordinary mortals. But this is not a tradition with very long standing; until relatively recently almost every male monarch to sit on the British throne was, from a moral point of view, a pretty poor role model.

Monarchs tended to get round the problem by being as discreet as possible about their many mistresses and affairs, thereby giving the general public the impression that royalty lived by the highest standards. Edward VII is a case in point – he happily slept with his friends' wives and at any one time he had four or five mistresses on the go.

Charles II was even more profligate – he had so many mistresses he named streets after them to keep them happy and made their children (his illegitimate offspring) dukes, earls and lords.

Visitors to St James's will discover that at least one street still bears the name of one of Charles II's favourite mistresses. This is Cleveland Row, a narrow street of eighteenth-century houses named after Barbara Palmer, Countess of Castlemaine, later Duchess of Cleveland.

Other, similarly dedicated streets have long vanished, as has a street named after one of the king's favourite snacks. Pickled Egg Walk, now Crawford Walk, was renamed in the nineteenth century, but it is commemorated in the Pickled Egg Tavern where Charles is supposed to have stopped regularly for a treat he apparently found irresistible (though some say the egg-lover was actually his father, Charles I).

BLACK BRICKS IN OLD QUEEN STREET

No. 26 Old Queen Street in Westminster is a beautiful Georgian house which – a rare thing these days – has kept at least some of its Georgian interiors. It lies on a road that runs into an even older street – Queen Anne's Gate – which is arguably the most beautiful street in London.

But No. 26 is interesting and rather special for the oddest of reasons.

Its strangeness dates back to a time before the Clean Air Acts of the 1950s and 1960s that banned the use of coal for domestic heating. The idea was to rid London of its wonderfully atmospheric but dangerous and unhealthy pea-souper fogs. These fogs, made famous by Whistler and other artists who saw romance and mystery in the murky gloom, caused thousands of deaths each year among the elderly and already ill.

The fog also ensured that almost every house in London quickly turned black after being built – so much so that it became fashionable to have a house with black bricks, ideally just the right shade of 'soot black'.

After the Second World War, when the Prime Minister's house at No. 10 Downing Street was altered, it was decided to clean the external bricks. The result looked so awful that the bricks were immediately painted black to recreate the dirty look they'd had before. And, to this day, the bricks of No. 10 are always painted black.

No. 26 Old Queen Street is rather similar, but its bricks are kept black by being washed in a special solution that is filled with genuine coal dust. The work is carried out by English Heritage which tries, against overwhelming odds, to protect the few interesting old buildings left in London.

No. 26 is interesting for another reason, too, for this was once the house in which the monarch's falconer lived. This was a highly prestigious job because falconry really was the sport of kings and was taken very seriously at least until the end of the eighteenth century. The king's falconer was so important that he was the only person besides the royal family itself allowed to drive along Birdcage Walk, which runs just behind Old Queen Street.

THE LAST OF
DEVIL'S ACRE

Modern visitors are often astonished to discover that one of the worst, most insanitary and over-crowded areas of London a century and more ago is now one of the most expensive and fashionable.

The area around Westminster Abbey and the House of Commons was once known as Devil's Acre. The name was a reflection of the endless narrow streets of small, badly built and disease-ridden houses that ran from Westminster down towards Victoria Station in one direction and towards Vauxhall Bridge in the other.

A clue to the former poverty of this area can be found in the vast numbers of flats that now exist in the Tachbrook and Peabody housing estates just a stone's throw from Parliament Square, which are still inhabited in many cases by the descendants of those who lived in Westminster's slums a century and more ago.

It may seem as if none of the small houses that were once typical of this area survive, but in fact some do. A short walk from Parliament Square leads you to Gayfere Street. Here you will see three very small, third-rate houses of a kind that once ran in every direction. Smartened up and lived in by the super-rich today, they are nonetheless a reminder of what this part of London once looked like. Another, similar example can be found in Old Queen Street, a narrow, pedestrianised alleyway that runs off Storey's Gate near Westminster Abbey. Here two tiny late seventeenth-century houses survive, crammed in and over-awed by later buildings. And if you visit Strutton Ground, about half a mile down Victoria Street from Parliament Square, you will see a few more examples of the sort of houses that once made up the heart of Devil's Acre.

SCANDAL AT THE
HORSE GUARDS

❧❦❧

If you stand on Horse Guards Parade, that magnificent square that leads to Whitehall on one side
and St James's Park on the other, you instantly notice
the white buildings straight ahead of you with their
central archway (built by the great Classical architect
Inigo Jones) but look to the right and there is an
equally distinguished-looking, white, stone-fronted
building with a prominent Venetian window. At one
time the Scotland Office (staffed by civil servants responsible for Scottish affairs), this building was originally a private residence.

Built in the 1750s for Sir Matthew Fetherstonhaugh
(pronounced 'Fanshaw'), the house was later occupied by Lord Montagu (at which time it became
Montagu House); it was owned from 1788 to 1792
by Frederick Duke of York, and from 1793 till 1830 by
Lord Melbourne.

It was at this point in the building's history, more
than two centuries ago, that one of the great scandals
of London life took place.

Lord Melbourne's son William had married Lady
Caroline Lamb who, on reading a new bestselling
poem called 'Childe Harold's Pilgrimage' (by Lord
Byron) declared that whatever the young poet looked
like she simply had to meet him.

And meet him she did. He almost certainly declared

his love for her in this house in Whitehall, possibly in the famous rotunda – a large, ornate, circular entrance hall unique in London and largely unaltered today.

What Caroline didn't realise, however, was that Byron's protestations of love did not mean he would stay with her forever. Their passionate affair ended in a welter of recrimination and insult that became far worse when Byron married Lady Caroline's cousin, Annabella Milbanke. Caroline must have thought she was extremely unlucky because Byron was a notorious rake and her husband William seems to have been even worse. (Indeed, in a letter to her mother Caroline implied that he made unreasonable and unnatural sexual demands.)

But Caroline and Byron's rows continued for years here in this house in Whitehall and elsewhere, reaching a pitch of intensity when she cut off all her pubic hair and sent it to him.

By 1830, the mad rants of Lady Caroline and her lover had long gone and the house had been renamed Dover House after its last private owner George James Welbore Agar-Ellis (Lord Dover). From 1830 until today Dover House has been the home of civil servants quietly devoted to Scottish affairs.

CUTTING THE RIBBON

❧❦❧

The long tradition of opening new buildings, shows and events by cutting a ribbon has its origins in London's long vanished Cloth Fair.

Cloth Fair was a medieval fair that took place each year for three days, starting at the end of St Bartholomew's Day (24 August).

The Fair was held on the Smoothfield (Smithfield is a corruption of the original name) just outside the old city gates and it was the place where merchants met to buy and sell cloth.

The fair was always opened by the Lord Mayor of London, who ceremoniously cut a piece of cloth to indicate that trading had begun, and this is why, centuries after the fair came to an end, we still cut a ribbon to ceremoniously open events.

The land around St Bartholomew's Church where Cloth Fair was held was owned by Lord Rich's family. Rich has gone down in history as the man who perjured himself to ensure that Thomas More was executed for refusing to acknowledge that Henry VIII was head of the church in England.

The houses in the little lane that is now known as Cloth Fair included, until 1917, several houses that dated from Lord Rich's time, but alas they were swept away at the end of the First World War. Two heavily restored seventeenth-century houses remain. Interestingly, one or two drapers and cloth merchants remained here until the beginning of the twentieth century.

LISTED PRISON BRICKS

One of the strangest and most remarkable structures ever to be erected in London was the
Millbank Prison. It was Europe's largest prison and
the huge area it covered included the site where Tate
Britain now stands near Vauxhall Bridge.

The idea for the prison originated with the philosopher Jeremy Bentham, who put forward proposals
for what he called his 'Panopticon Prison' – its basic
design premise was that one guard could observe
(-opticon) all (pan-) the inmates at the same time.

In practice, of course, even though the guard would
be seated as it were at the centre of a spider's web of
corridors and cells, he would not actually be able to
see every cell at the same time but none of the prisoners could ever be sure that their cell was not the one
being looked at.

Other than saving money on prison warders it is
hard to know why Bentham thought this was a particularly useful idea, but then Bentham was an eccentric
who famously asked that after death his body be sent
to a taxidermist and his preserved remains propped up
in a glass case at University College London, which
he had helped to found. But he thought the sense that
they were always being watched would 'grind rogues
into honest fellows'.

Bentham's ideas were abandoned before the prison
was built but they influenced the bizarre edifice that

went up a decade later. The new architect was clearly aware of Bentham's proposal because some aspects of the spider's web idea were incorporated.

The eccentricities of the whole idea of a Millbank prison continued, however, when it was discovered that the man given the task of designing it was a former art master with no experience of building at all. His drawings were so bizarre that it took three genuine architects to make sense of them and, over the following decade, get the job finished.

The prison had a central block with six sides, and going away from this block were separate blocks that could only be reached through the main hub in the middle. The result was a building that looked like a giant snowflake.

Despite the enormous amounts of time and money spent on it, Millbank Prison began to sink into the river mud almost from the day it was completed. The foundations were inadequate for such a huge building and one, moreover, that had been built on permanently soggy ground.

The nearness of the filthy river also meant that prisoners died from frequent outbreaks of disease; so many that eventually a new prison was built on higher ground at Pentonville in north London and Millbank was kept only for those prisoners awaiting transportation to Australia – a role Millbank continued to fill until demolition began in 1892.

Everyone whose ancestors were transported from England to Australia between 1840 and 1890 would have walked down the river steps from the prison, stepped on to a boat and vanished probably forever down the Thames and across the ocean.

But one extraordinary thing rose from the ruins of

the prison. For centuries this had been a very poor part of London – it was an extension, if you like, of the Devil's Acre slum area of nearby Westminster – so a decision was made to reuse the millions of bricks from the prison to build more than 4,000 working people's flats.

These flats comprise the Millbank Estate, which can still be seen here, hardly altered since first built. Indeed, so well made are the flats that they are now listed as of special historic interest by English Heritage. Also, as a nice touch, the flats were named after famous English painters, including Turner and Hogarth.

Nearby and also listed is the old Army Medical College building where the world's first effective typhoid vaccine was discovered. Set around a square where the soldiers once paraded, the college buildings are now used by an art college, but they have not been in the least spoiled or hacked about by show-off architects obsessed with livening things up with steel and glass.

A few other traces of the old prison remain. On the edge of the Millbank flats nearest Vauxhall Bridge Road there is what looks like a deep ditch running for perhaps 100 yards – this is the last section of the perimeter ditch from the original prison. On the riverside nearby is one other remnant of the old prison; a heavy stone bollard which once stood at the top of the river steps from which so many prisoners departed England. It is said that the prisoners would brush their hand across the top of the bollard as they went down the steps to the boats. A last touch of England.

THE WONDERS
OF THE POST

❦

The early-nineteenth-century General Post Office at St Martin's le Grand near St Paul's Cathedral was a monument to one of the wonders of the age – an institution that would deliver a letter next day to any part of the United Kingdom. This huge achievement deserved a magnificent building, which is why Sir Robert Smirke was commissioned to design the huge Neoclassical building that once stood on this prime site in the city.

But the general post office had existed for far longer. In fact, it is the oldest in the world, having carried mail since around 1640. In the early years, its London premises tended to move about and it is known to have been based at three City addresses in earlier times, including Cloak Hill near Dowgate Hill.

Early post was paid for by the person receiving the mail rather than the person sending it – which created the odd situation whereby if the person to whom a letter was addressed did not want to receive the letter (or if he simply didn't want to pay) he could refuse to hand over his money and the post office would have to take the letter back and absorb the cost of having transported it perhaps halfway across the country for no reason.

The introduction of the penny post in the mid-nineteenth century ended this state of affairs and letter writing suddenly boomed, aided no doubt by growing literacy levels among the middle classes and even the better-off working classes.

In London at the end of the nineteenth century, a letter posted in the morning to another address in the capital might well reach its destination by late afternoon and, in the capital at least, there were as many as eight deliveries and collections each day.

Smirke's wonderful building was 400 feet long and the hub of this wonderful system of communication. It opened in 1829 but by 1910 was deemed too small and it was demolished in 1912.

Not a trace remains unless, bizarrely, you fancy a trip to Vestry Road, Walthamstow on the north-eastern fringes of London. Here, halfway along the road, is the top half of a massive Ionic pillar – in surprisingly good condition. It looks absurd amidst the small houses nearby, but is the last vestige of Smirke's magnificent Georgian General Post Office, the first purpose-built post office building in the world.

BLOW-UP BRIDGE

❧❦❧

The pillars on Blow-Up Bridge, which crosses the Regent's Canal near London Zoo, are the first thing the passing walker (or canal barge passenger) notices. Immensely thick and made from cast iron, they seem almost too robust for the narrow brick bridge they support. These pillars, however, are the only remnants of the first bridge that crossed the canal at this point – a bridge, moreover, that was blown up in one of the biggest explosions the capital has ever experienced.

To understand how the accident happened we have to remember that the pretty tree-lined canal we see today is a relatively recent phenomenon. For almost 150 years after they were dug, England's canals were grimy industrial corridors through the landscape. Their sole purpose was to move heavy goods from one industrial part of the country to another. They did this very cheaply and very efficiently – so much so that there are plans to return them, in a limited way, to their original use.

The Grand Union and Regent's Canals were among the most important of these watery highways. Massive loads could be moved very cheaply on barges pulled by one or two horses. Once the horses got the barge moving, its momentum would help keep it going, so canals were cut from the Thames up to Birmingham, Manchester and beyond.

It might seem a slow process but it was cheap, with the bargees living with their families in tiny rooms at one end of their long narrowboats and the rest of the boat piled high with coal, steel or pottery.

Then, on a fateful day in 1874, a barge loaded to the gunwales with gunpowder passed under what was then known as Macclesfield Bridge. No one knows precisely what ignited the powder, but the resultant explosion was heard across the whole of London. 'It was like a deep thump that moved the ground,' recalled someone living in the notorious potteries district of North Kensington, some four miles away.

The explosion destroyed the bridge and of course hardly a scrap of the boat or its inhabitants could later be found, but the massive cast-iron pillars were recovered – one or two from the canal and at least one from a field more than 100 yards away. The pillars were reused in the bridge we see today and if you look carefully you will see that they were put back the wrong way around. The deepest grooves cut by the ropes that had pulled the barges are now on the towpath side of the pillars rather than on the canal side where they should be.

BUILT ON WATER

The church of St John's Waterloo is unique among London churches in that it is largely held up by muddy water. This may make it sound as if this is a church that should be avoided if you wish to escape having tons of rubble collapsing on your head, but paradoxically the muddy water has made the church one of the most stable in London.

To find out why it was built on water we need to go back to the early nineteenth century when London was expanding rapidly as the industrial revolution drew in hundreds of thousands of people from rural areas. Parliament, always far more concerned with the spiritual nourishment of its citizens than with their physical welfare, decided more churches were needed for this increased population, so the Commissioners for New Buildings voted £64,000, an enormous sum at the time, for a new church to be built on the road leading to Waterloo Bridge.

The decision to build St John's was taken in 1822 and the building completed in 1824. Curiously, and despite the growing passion for the Gothic style, the architect chosen for the new church was a Greek scholar, the splendidly named Francis Octavius Bedford. Not surprisingly he insisted on building a Greek Revival church and no sooner had it opened than it was subject to a torrent of abuse from modernisers who insisted it should have been built in the newly fashionable Gothic style.

The church may have been unfashionable from the outset, but the architect had the sense to consult the great engineer John Rennie the Younger (1794–1874) before starting work. The problem was that this part of London was deep marsh. However far down the engineers dug they found only oozing mud and then water. In those pre-concrete days, a solid raft could not easily be built as it would be for a tower block or other structure today, so Rennie suggested a solution that the Romans and other, much earlier builders had relied on: he proposed driving long oak piles – in essence sharpened tree trunks – deep into the mud below where the church walls were to be built.

It was known at the time that oak used in this way could easily last thousands of years. A well preserved oak pile from the Roman river embankment had recently been discovered – it is now preserved in the entrance porch of the church of St Magnus the Martyr at the north end of London Bridge.

But it was still a risk. Rennie's confidence, however, inspired Bedford and his plan worked brilliantly – at least until twentieth-century work disturbed the extraordinary balance between oak and water that had supported the massive stone church for so long. Even a direct hit by a bomb in 1940 only damaged the roof and interior. The walls on their springy base bounced back and were used in the restoration of the church, whereas other church walls on solid foundations had to be demolished after bomb damage.

In the 1970s and 1980s, the Underground Jubilee Line tunnel was built under and close by the church and the ground, waterlogged for thousands of years, began to dry out. The church quickly became unstable and had the drying-out continued it would have collapsed. The solution was to restore the watery base that, combined with ancient oak, had preserved the church for so long. So, millions of gallons of river water were pumped back into and around the church foundations. The result once again is a remarkably sound building which should stand for a thousand years.

NIGHTINGALE'S OWL

※

Florence Nightingale is deservedly famous as the founder of modern nursing. Born into a privileged, wealthy home, she had to fight to be allowed to work at all in an age when to do nothing was considered the only proper occupation for a middle-class woman.

She, more than anyone in the nineteenth century, understood the need for hygiene and clean air in hospitals. She became so influential that when St Thomas's Hospital moved to Lambeth in the mid-nineteenth century she was largely responsible for the courtyard design of the wards, a design that ensured maximum light and air for the wards.

Today, one of London's most unusual museums is dedicated to her life and work. It is located in the hospital where so many of her ideas were and are embodied. Here you can see Nightingale's best friend preserved forever by a taxidermist. Eccentrically, her best friend was a little owl called Athena. She had discovered Athena as an abandoned chick in Athens (hence the name) and using her nursing skills kept the tiny bird alive when it was at the brink of death. It thrived, became an adult bird and refused for the rest of its life to leave her side. Wherever and whenever she travelled, Athena went with her in a specially enlarged pocket in her dress.

When Athena died she was sent to the taxidermist and as a result looks today just as she looked in life. The museum is also home to the slate on which Florence Nightingale learned to write as a child.

A statue of the famous nurse can be seen at St Thomas's too, but this is a copy of the original, which was stolen in 1970. The statue would not have been valuable and it was so famous that any thief trying to sell it would have been immediately arrested, so its disappearance remains a mystery. One theory is that an admirer of Nightingale simply had to have it and it remains in his collection but well out of sight of the public.

QUEEN IN A CELLAR

One of the greatest architectural losses in London was the destruction in the early nineteenth century of the church of St Dunstan-in-the-West. The church that existed at that time dated back to the tenth and eleventh centuries. It escaped the Great Fire of 1666 through the quick thinking of the Dean of Westminster, who woke dozens of schoolboys in the middle of the night, formed them into a chain and got them to throw buckets of water over the flames as they approached the church along Fleet Street where the fire, though still burning, did not rage quite as it did at the other end of the street closer to the City proper.

The nineteenth-century obsession with updating and rebuilding London's churches destroyed this remarkable structure and the architect John Shaw (and his son, also John) was employed to rebuild the church in 1831. During rebuilding a remarkable discovery was made and it would not have happened at that time or perhaps ever if the church had not been demolished. A statue of Queen Elizabeth I was found buried nearby and today this is the only statue of the queen in London and the only statue of her known to have been carved during her lifetime. It probably stood originally in a niche in nearby Ludgate, the entrance to the City from the west. Other treasures in the church include numerous monuments saved and refixed from the earlier church and the world-famous clock on the wall outside, high above Fleet Street. The clock dates back to the 1670s.

RAG-BAG CHURCH

One of the curious things about the City of London's churches is that many of those that survive are actually recreations from the 1950s. So many German bombs were dropped on London during the Second World War that hardly a church escaped unscathed. Many were burned out by fire bombs, their blackened walls and towers the only survivors of the flames.

But, sadly, many churches were also demolished in the nineteenth and early twentieth centuries by the Church of England, which refused to see its buildings as anything other than a financial burden. Some of the oldest and least-altered churches were lost in this way.

But the artefacts from many churches – both those bombed and those demolished – were often saved and moved to other churches. One of the most impressive rag-bag churches that received masses of material from other churches also happens to be one of the very few that was not damaged during the war: St Margaret Lothbury.

Two paintings in the church – of Moses and Aaron – come from the long-vanished church of St Christopher le Stocks in Threadneedle Street, which was demolished as long ago as 1781. This church once housed the magnificent bust of Sir Peter Lemaire that you can see on the north wall of St Margaret's; the font, communion rails and reredos are from St Olave,

Old Jewry, along with a very rare sword rest and some beautiful marble monuments. The choir screen and pulpit sounding board came from All-Hallows-the-Great in Thames Street, which was demolished in 1894.

In fact, St Margaret's has the great distinction of including substantial remnants of no few than seven other parish churches.

FAT BERG TOUR

The Abbey Mills pumping station in Stratford East is a magnificent, half Italian Renaissance, half Gothic monument to one of the greatest engineers Britain has ever produced.

Sir Joseph Bazalgette created the sewage system on which London still relies. At a time when millions of tons of untreated sewage entered the River Thames each year, he designed and helped build an extraordinary network of gigantic sewers that carry most of London's waste to Beckton, a huge sewage treatment centre where it is all cleaned and then released into the Thames Estuary. But what makes Abbey Mills really unusual is that you can apply for a tour of the building that includes a visit to the sewers themselves.

Bazalgette himself appears to have walked almost every yard of his new sewer system and even today the 6-foot diameter tunnels are a marvel of intricate brick work, for these sewers had to be built without the benefits of concrete (yet to be invented).

Cleverly, Bazalgette designed his system in such a way that raw sewage was always diluted by rainwater runoff and bathwater, so the experience of walking the tunnels is not so dreadful as it might otherwise be. Bazalgette was also an extraordinary visionary. He calculated the maximum amount of sewage he thought each Londoner would produce each year and used that to calculate the diameter of his sewer tunnels. Then, to allow for future population growth, he decided to double all his calculations – the result was a system that has lasted largely unaltered to this day.

But some things about the sewer system might well have surprised even Bazalgette.

Wonderfully efficient though they are, the sewers regularly produce something that might have been invented by science fiction writers; not giant rats (rodents are in fact virtually unheard of in the system as the water levels are too high), nor dead bodies, but 'fat bergs'. These may sound harmless enough but they can be as big as a double-decker bus. One fat berg – an accumulation of fat from cooking waste – that was discovered in the sewers under Leicester Square was equivalent to six double-decker buses. So if you take the tour – beware!

PEPYS'S WALKWAY

⁓⁕⁓

St Olave Hart Street is one of only a few medieval churches that survive in the City. It is also
the city's smallest church. Unfortunately, like so many
London churches, its interior was largely destroyed by
a German firebomb. But the church still has much of
interest, including a mark on the wall that reveals the
location of a long bricked-up door built specially by
the great seventeenth-century diarist Samuel Pepys,
who worshipped here with his wife Elisabeth. Both
are buried in the churchyard here. Pepys by his own
admission slept through many services, but he liked
to attend church to ogle any young women who happened to be there. In fact, one young woman resented
this so much that she stuck a pin in him.

Pepys worked at the Navy Board nearby and he
hated to get wet, so he had a covered way, staircase
and door built so he could get from his desk to his
pew in one of the St Olave's galleries (long gone)
without having to go outside and risk the weather.

Another curious tale from St Olave's (the church
is named after a Norwegian saint) concerns William
Penn, the father of the founder of Pennsylvania. Penn
spotted that St Olave's was in danger of being burned
during the Great Fire, so he roused dozens of men
from the naval dockyards nearby and they pulled
down the houses surrounding the church, an act that
saved it from destruction.

SCHOOL FOR SCANDAL

Few private houses in London have such a rich and strange history as Walpole House in Chiswick.

Built in the late seventeenth century, the house looks out across a narrow riverside street to the Thames. In its early days it provided a home for Barbara Villiers (1640–1709) for the last nine years of her life. She had been the great beauty of the age and among Charles II's favourite mistresses. After his death in 1685, a Puritan air settled on London and Villiers found herself banished from court. She was unhappy and decided in her final years to come here to Chiswick, which was then a deeply unfashionable village, miles from London.

Soon after she took up residence in the house, local residents regularly reported seeing her praying at an upstairs window by the light of the moon and, whatever the truth of the story, it is certain that she was a sad, embittered woman in her last years. She could never accept the loss of her beauty, nor the loss of her position at court.

She died here at Walpole House and her unhappiness was so great that it was said her ghost was regularly seen at the window, and even into the twentieth century residents of the house occasionally reported hearing footsteps crossing empty rooms late at night.

But Walpole House has other claims to fame.

Thomas Walpole, nephew of the Prime Minister Sir Robert, lived here from 1798 to 1803 and by the mid-nineteenth century it was a school for vagrant girls. The school became very well known – so much so that it was even visited by Queen Victoria.

By the 1840s, Walpole House had changed hands again. It was now a boys' school where the author William Thackeray studied for a while and it was this building (so it is claimed) that he immortalised as the dreadful Miss Pinkerton's Academy in his famous novel *Vanity Fair*.

LEAPFROGGING BISHOP

❦

Edward Hervey (1730–1803) joined the church because he wanted a job that paid well but involved almost no work. His brother was the Bishop of London, so when Edward was offered the bishopric of Boyne in Ireland, he took it. A little later he was offered the even more lucrative bishopric of Derry, so he took that too.

Fed up with Ireland, he eventually became Bishop of Bristol but lived in London and employed someone else (on a pittance) to carry out his ecclesiastical duties in the West Country.

Hervey was very eccentric and he had a particular love for leapfrog, which he insisted the junior clergy join in.

While in London, he tried to persuade the Bishop of Southwark to introduce a rule that all future Bishops should have to play leapfrog at least once a year. His fellow bishop was appalled at the suggestion and refused. Hervey was indignant and left Britain for several years to travel in style and at great expense across Europe.

POWDER MAGAZINE

Buildings used to store gunpowder were known as magazines. They were usually, though by no means always, situated in remote areas because of the danger of explosions – modern nitro-powders are far less likely to be accidentally ignited, but 'black powder', as it is known, is extremely volatile.

Astonishingly, a gunpowder magazine still exists in central London. This is the Hyde Park magazine, situated on the north side of Rennie's beautiful stone bridge across the Serpentine. The distinctive Greek Revival-style building with its columned portico was completed in 1805 and there is no doubt that one of the main reasons it was built here was that Hyde Park had long been (and still remains) a place of popular protest. If a popular rising had to be suppressed using firearms then it might well happen in Hyde Park, and that was the justification for building the magazine here.

Powder magazines of this type were built with very little metal – typically even the floorboards would be positioned using wooden dowels rather than nails in order to reduce the risk of a spark igniting the powder.

Remarkably, the Hyde Park magazine was still owned and run (as a general storeroom) well into the 1960s.

NOT JUST CHURCHES

O ne of the strangest historical remains in London must be the Standard Reservoir Conduit House at Greenwich. When one thinks of the great architect Nicholas Hawksmoor, who was responsible for such magnificent churches as Christ Church Spitalfields, one forgets that in addition to his church work Hawksmoor was Clerk of the Works at Greenwich Hospital in south London from 1698 to 1735.

He almost certainly built the conduit house that survives in Greenwich Park. It was built above a reservoir designed to supply the Royal Hospital for Seamen at Greenwich with fresh water. This was one of the earliest attempts to bring water by pipe (or conduit) to London.

The building is in remarkably good condition, but even more extraordinary is the 200-metre stretch of brick conduit tunnel that survives under the conduit house leading down towards the old hospital, which is now the National Maritime Museum.

The fine brown bricks and classical style of the conduit house belie its purely functional origins.

The walls include beautifully carved eighteenth-century graffiti, including the name of M Pinfold and the date 1770.

MEMBERS' LAMP

At the corner of Bridge Street and Parliament Square there is a stone pillar not unlike all the other stone pillars than run along the boundary of the Houses of Parliament, except that it is taller, and the observant will notice that it is topped with a curious glass lamp.

This lamp has been here since the days of horse-drawn hansom cabs and enables MPs to save time when they need a cab. They ring the Constable (as the relevant Palace of Westminster official is known) and tell him they will be leaving the office in, say, ten minutes. The Constable presses a button and the glass lamp starts to flash, telling any cab driver passing by that if he stops at the gate he will have the privilege of carrying an MP or minister home.

TIDE MACHINE

Centuries ago, the great houses that lined the Thames in the west of London, especially along the Strand, all had their own private access to the river. Rudimentary, unsurfaced roads meant that in winter especially they were so muddy they could not be used at all. The river, therefore, was a vital transport route and the watermen who rowed people up and down (and to Southwark and back) were an immensely important group of people.

Indeed, they were instrumental in slowing the rate at which bridges were built across the river, fearing that each bridge would reduce their importance and ability to make a living. They turned out to be right, as today the once numerous watermen have vanished.

When the various bridges were eventually built, ancient statutes ensured that steps down to the river had to be included in their structure, which is why in central London you find so many sets of granite steps leading down to the water's edge. They are hardly used since few wish to venture down on to the muddy river banks, but ancient laws ensured they were built. The steps are used today by a few intrepid anglers and treasure hunters who sieve the gravel at the river's edge looking for ancient coins and other artefacts.

One such set of steps can be found leading from the Embankment up to Westminster Bridge. If you look closely here, halfway up the steps and fixed on the stone parapet you will see a small octagonal room whose upper parts are made from copper sheet, with slits for windows and iron steps bolted on to its walls.

This little room, though now unused, was once a vital tool in flood control on the Thames or at least in trying to control the effects of an impending flood. The room formerly contained an elaborate and highly sophisticated piece of Victorian engineering – a mass of wheels and cogs designed to measure the height of the tide each day.

What was especially clever was that the height of the river was automatically recorded by a pen and a piece of paper attached to the machine – as the water rose and fell the pen moved at the dictates of the wheels and cogs and pinions to leave a precise record. Each evening the paper would be checked by someone from the Port of London Authority. Sadly the mechanism has gone but the little room that once housed it remains as a reminder of how important it was once for Londoners to know what the river was doing.

The need for the tide measurer vanished finally with the construction in the 1980s of the Thames Barrier, which regulates the height of the tides right across central London and up as far as Teddington.

SHOOTER'S HILL TOWER

~~~❦~~~

The late eighteenth and early nineteenth centuries saw the beginning of a massive growth of interest in the Gothic, or Gothick as it was often spelled, especially in architecture.

This development coincided with a huge shift in literature and the arts generally from the rational, highly structured and formal to a wilder, more Romantic style. The measured poetry of Alexander Pope and the other so-called Augustans gave place to the more emotional verse of Byron, Keats, Shelley and above all Wordsworth.

In architecture, the Gothic, hearkening back to a supposed medieval style, was seen as more English, a native tradition whose revival was justified on the grounds that Classical was somehow a foreign, un-English imposition.

Just as great landowners in the 1700s had built classically inspired houses and follies in their grounds – the supreme example being perhaps Chiswick House in west London – so Gothic houses and follies were now built, and few stranger than the curiously named Severndroog Castle on Shooter's Hill in Greenwich, south-east London.

Severndroog was designed by the little-known architect Richard Jupp and work started in 1784. It represents the embodiment of the early craze for Gothic and was commissioned by Lady James of

Eltham, widow of Commodore Sir William James who was famous in his day for the destruction of the fortress of Suvarnadurg in India in 1755. The British had attacked the fortress on the coast of India on the grounds that it was held by Tulaji Angre, someone they considered a pirate.

Lady James's monument to her husband is a most curious piece of architecture. More than sixty feet high and built in good-quality brown bricks, the castle is triangular but has a hexagonal turret at each corner. It is as far from the restrained classical style of half a century earlier as can be imagined.

Lady James chose this particular style of monument in part at least because she wanted a viewing point and this site was ideal – on a clear day the northern hills of London are clearly visible from the tower, as well as much of Sussex and Kent, the Thames Estuary and Essex.

Lady James appears to have lost interest in her castle as the eighteenth century neared its end. She allowed the installation of a theodolite at the top of the tower in the 1780s as part of a trigonometric survey – and it was this survey that led eventually to the formation of the world-famous Ordnance Survey, the first ever systematic mapping of the United Kingdom.

BLACK ROD'S BOYS

The office of Black Rod, or (to give it its full name) the Gentleman Usher of the Black Rod, is well known; at the State Opening of Parliament he walks from the House of Lords to the House of Commons and has the door slammed in his face for his pains. The slamming of the door symbolises the lower house's independence from the Lords and the monarchy.

Having knocked on the door three times with his ebony (black) rod, he is allowed to enter in order to summon the Commons to the Lords' chamber to hear the Queen's Speech. But Black Rod has other duties – he can arrest any lord who misbehaves (very rare) and he is also responsible for the buildings and security of the Palace of Westminster (as the Houses of Lords and Commons are known collectively). Black Rod has one final and rather odd duty. Each year he is obliged to organise a tea party for the children attending nearby Westminster School. The tea party is held, appropriately enough, in Black Rod's Garden.

At the top of a short flight of steps leading from the terrace of the Palace of Westminster down to the River Thames, there is a small pavilion, which was built in 1860. The steps to this pavilion are known as Black Rod's Steps and the pavilion is situated in what is known as Black Rod's Garden. For centuries, schoolboys from Westminster have been permitted to land at Black Rod's Steps and once a year a small group of these extraordinarily lucky children arrive at the steps for tea on the House of Lords terrace.

QUEEN ANNE'S ALCOVE

At the Bayswater end of the Serpentine in Hyde Park is a curious shelter. Immensely tall and built of carefully cut stone, the shelter, which is open to the elements on one side, has fine oak panelling and a curved wooden seat.

Many visitors sit here to enjoy the view across the ornamental ponds and fountains nearby but few realise that this unaltered and rather magnificent little building dates back to 1705.

At that time, it was situated a few hundred yards away, near Kensington Palace, but it was felt to attract too many prostitutes and plans were hatched to get rid of it. Outraged by this, a London builder called Mr Cowley, who loved the summerhouse, had it moved in 1867 to its present location. He paid for the move out of his own pocket and we should be grateful to him because without his action the summerhouse would almost certainly have been demolished.

The move took the structure away from the strait-laced royals in their grand palace and placed it on the edge of Hyde Park, well away from Kensington Palace.

With its triangular pediment and twin alcoves (as well as Queen Anne's monogram), the summerhouse is rather grand, but what makes it even more remarkable is that it may well have been designed by the great Sir Christopher Wren and is perhaps his least-known building.

WHAT'S IN A NAME?

One of London's most ancient thoroughfares, the Strand – meaning a stretch of land by the water – was once the site of numerous mansions and palaces. It was just half a mile or so from the entrance to the City of London at Ludgate, but far enough away to allow the aristocracy to enjoy the fresh air and open space – and there was less risk of contracting the plague here on its periodic arrivals in the dense and crowded city.

One aristocrat who owned land along the Strand was George Villiers, 2nd Duke of Buckingham (1628–87). Villiers was part of the 'Merry Gang', which included the most notorious rake of the Restoration era, John Wilmot, 2nd Earl of Rochester. Villiers was an amusing man but constantly fighting and womanising, to the extent that he was on several occasions imprisoned in the Tower of London. Each time he was released because Charles II enjoyed his company and had spent some of his time in exile in the company of Villiers.

When Villiers needed money, which, with his gambling and womanising, he frequently did – he sold his possessions. Eventually, he sold his house and land along the Strand. York House, a grand residence overlooking the Thames, had been owned by the Villiers family for generations. It stood facing the Thames, just to the east of where Charing Cross Station now stands.

Villiers sold up but could not bear the idea that his name would be forgotten in the area, so the builder who planned to demolish York House and lay out a new grid of streets was told that one condition of the sale was that every part of the duke's name had to be incorporated into the new street names.

This is the reason that today you will find a street running down the side of Charing Cross Station called Villiers Street. Nearby you will also find George Street, Buckingham Street and Duke Street. Villiers also had to have a little fun and when he saw that the word 'of' (remember, his full title was 'George Villiers, Duke of Buckingham') had not been included in the street names, he insisted that the deal was off unless there was a road or street called 'Of'. A compromise was reached and a narrow alley off Villiers Street became and remained until recently 'Of Alley'. It was renamed York Place in the twentieth century, but after a huge campaign of protest the sign carrying the new name also included the line 'Formerly Of Alley'.

RABBIT-PROOF
FENCE

Many people forget that until well into the 1960s London's Royal Parks still had a population of rabbits, and signs in Kensington Gardens still explained that it was forbidden to annoy the sheep in the park.

The rabbits that inhabited the parks may well have been descendants of rabbits introduced and carefully protected in the Middle Ages. At this time, no grand menu was complete without a dish that included rabbit, which was eaten only by the very wealthy. But by the eighteenth century, rabbits had spread far and wide and, because everyone could now eat them, the rich lost interest. Indeed, rabbits had become pests and the carefully protected warrens where they had once been allowed to breed unhindered became things of the past. However, despite this change in status, some rabbits did survive in the Royal Parks, and proof that they were once there can be seen in the design of the eighteenth-century railings that run along the backs of the old houses in Birdcage Walk opposite St James's Park.

If you look carefully, you will see that the six-foot-high railings have much shorter spikes between their main spikes. These are perhaps two feet high and their purpose was to reduce the gap between the main spikes so that rabbits couldn't pass through them. Just because rabbits still ran around in St James's Park, the gardeners in these grand houses did not want their carefully tended plants to be eaten by starving bunnies.

LEANING BEN

❧

Big Ben is perhaps the most famous symbol of London, far more evocative of the capital than the London Eye, or even the red bus. Big Ben was originally known as St Stephen's Tower, then the Clock Tower, before finally being renamed Elizabeth Tower in honour of Queen Elizabeth II's Diamond Jubilee. These names, however, have always been ignored to some extent, as the clock tower is really always referred to as Big Ben, which is actually the name of its biggest bell. Only in Wales is at least one of the tower's official names still used – in Welsh, the Elizabeth II Tower and Parliament as a whole is still known as '*San Steffan*'.

Despite its fame, the 315ft-high tower has a rather sinister history. Indeed, the difficulties of designing it drove Augustus Pugin to madness and death. Already overworked by the need to create thousands of designs for other parts of the Palace of Westminster, Pugin, the archpriest of the new Gothic style, was exhausted by the time he finished the drawings for the tower and he never recovered.

Another bizarre feature of the tower is that only UK citizens may visit the interior. This can only be arranged through one's MP and there is a long waiting list. There is also no lift, so the tower can only be climbed via more than 300 stone steps.

One final curious fact about Big Ben is that it leans more than nine inches to the north-west and, depending on the weather and temperature, it moves slowly back and forth as the year progresses and the weather gets gradually warmer and then colder!

A BIRD AT THE
CORONATION

❦

Osborne de Vere Beauclerk, 12th Duke of St Albans, inherited his title as a direct result of the fact that his ancestor, Nell Gwyn (often, and wrongly, spelled Gwynn), gave birth to an illegitimate son of Charles II. Legend has it that the Dukedom was created for the fourteen-year-old Charles Beauclerk after his mother, in the king's presence, shouted: 'Come here and see your father, you little bastard!' Charles thought this was a dreadful insult, so he gave his son a very grand title indeed. Thus are great families born.

In fact, Charles felt so guilty about having so many illegitimate sons that he made them all dukes and earls – the Earldoms Richmond, Grafton and Lennox were all created in this way.

The 12th Duke of St Albans was a wonderful eccentric. He spent part of his final years travelling around America on a Greyhound bus and caused a scandal when Queen Elizabeth II was crowned in 1953.

Having discovered that he held the hereditary office of Master Falconer, the Duke told the organisers of the coronation that he would be attending the ceremony, as was his right, and he would also be carrying a live falcon. When the officials protested that this was absurd, the Duke pointed out that not only was he coming with a falcon, but it was his duty as laid down in statute to do so.

Panic ensued and a compromise was finally reached when the Duke agreed to attend the coronation with a bird – but it would be stuffed rather than alive.

So eccentric was the duke – and so grand – that when not attending royal weddings he went several times a week to his club in St James's Street to find an underling who could wind his watch for him.

HERB STREWER

Until the end of the nineteenth century, London and its inhabitants stank. Visitors were shocked at the state of the streets, the smell of the drains and cesspits and the rank odours that rose from over-filled parish churchyards, where the dead were often left just inches under the soil.

Monarchs of course were protected to some extent from the worst street smells, and since they could afford unlimited amounts of perfume they were at least able to disguise their own lack of hygiene. (Baths were considered eccentric and even dangerous until the end of the eighteenth century.)

Pomanders of various sorts were carried by the rich when they travelled in litters or carriages through the streets of London. Often these would be oranges spiked with cloves and were wafted under the nose.

As part of the general attempt to protect themselves from noxious odours, the royal family, at some time in the sixteenth or seventeenth centuries, decided to create the post of 'Herb Strewer'.

The first herb strewer for whom there is any record was Bridget Rumney, who, as her title suggests, strewed herbs for more than a decade in the royal apartments for Charles II, for the princely sum of £12 per year plus two yards of scarlet cloth.

When George III was crowned in 1760, Mary Dowle was there to throw scented herbs in front of the royal entourage and the tradition was still going strong in 1820 when George IV was crowned.

The title seems to have become hereditary by this time, so it may be that Mary Dowle died childless, as the next herb strewer on record is one Anne Fellowes. She was appointed by George IV just before his coronation. By this time, holders of the title had gone from being lowly servants to being rather grand friends of the monarch, but the title as a practical job seems to have died with George IV, since no coronation since his has included the services of a herb strewer. However, the Fellowes family are certain that the title remains with them and it is given to the eldest daughter in each generation.

MULTIPLE GEORGES

Pratt's Club is based in a narrow, terraced house in Park Place, just off St James's Street, and it is surely one of the oddest private members' clubs in the world. It reputedly has around 600 members, yet has room for only fourteen at any one time around the single, tiny dining table in the basement. The club was not founded by a group of aristocrats or members of the same trade. Indeed, the house where the club is based was once the home of Nathaniel Pratt, a servant employed as steward by the Duke of Beaufort.

The club began when Beaufort and a few friends dropped in on the steward one evening in the 1850s and had so much fun they kept coming back. By 1857, the club existed formally and began to take new members. But, despite the growth in membership, they couldn't bear to move and find new, bigger premises.

Even today, therefore, the club still only has two rooms – the aforementioned dining room and a small sitting room. There is a billiard room, too, but it is apparently only used to store members' coats!

The club is marvellously old fashioned – there is no central heating and no lift, despite the advanced average age of the members and the 100 and more steps from the basement to the top of the house.

But Pratt's greatest claim to fame is the bizarre tradition concerning its staff. All the male staff for as long as anyone can remember have been called

George, and if you apply for a job at Pratt's today you still have to agree – as one of the conditions of service – to be called George.

The tradition is believed to have started because Pratt's members were so habitually drunk that they could never remember the real names of their servants and all resorted to 'George' to save confusion.

A difficulty arose when the Club employed its first waitress. The problem was quickly solved when they decided to call her Georgina.

GARDEN OF EARTHLY
DELIGHTS

Buckingham Palace is one of the most famous
buildings in the world and its history is well
known. Less well known, however, is its garden, which
extends to forty-two acres – the biggest in London –
and has a remarkable wealth of wildlife, including an
extraordinary number of moth species.

Pride of place among the trees and plants is an ancient mulberry tree planted, it is said, during the reign
of James VI and I (1566–1625), which serves as a reminder of one of the oddest periods in English history.

When silk first reached England from China it
was considered such a wonderful material that plans
were quickly hatched to find the secret to how it was
made. Eventually it was discovered that the material
came from the silkworm, although when this was first
explained many scientists were outraged that anyone
could be fooled by such an unlikely explanation.

Eventually stories of silkworms were believed and
entrepreneurs began to hope it might be possible
to produce the wonderful new material in England.
Travellers were quizzed about silk making on the
other side of the world and the basic facts of the
business were pieced together. Key to any hope of
breeding and keeping silkworms was finding out what
they ate, and when it was realised that mulberry trees
were vital, a programme of frenzied planting began.

But, in their ignorance, those early plantsmen failed to realise that silkworms need white mulberry trees, not black mulberries. Almost all the mulberry trees planted in England in the early seventeenth century, including the one in the garden of Buckingham Palace, were the wrong type for silkworms, therefore, but they did produce the most wonderful fruit.

The other strange thing about Buckingham Palace is that the River Tyburn flows right underneath it!

CAB RULES

Until the 1950s it was still a requirement of London taxi drivers to keep a bag of hay somewhere in the cab. This may seem silly, but it was simply that the rules had not been changed since the last hansom cab had been licensed as recently as 1947. Hansoms were all horse-pulled cabs and for many elderly cab drivers they are a personal memory.

Add to that the fact that the old cab drivers' shelters were identical to the ones used at the end of the nineteenth century and it is easy to see why, in the world of the London cabby, things change slowly. This may also explain why the black cab we see today has hardly changed at all since its introduction. Even in the 1960s the space next to the driver was still open to the elements – it was where luggage had to be tied in with leather straps because the boot (in theory) still contained that bale of hay.

Some other, very strange cab-driving traditions survived into the 1970s. Until 1976, for example, all cabs had to be made so that the roof in the passengers' compartment was high enough to let an averaged-height man keep his top hat on.

And, to this day, it is perfectly legal for a cab driver to get out of his or her cab anywhere in London and urinate in broad daylight – just so long as he goes to the offside back of the cab to do it!

HEDGEHOG CONTROL

❧◈❧

Before the introduction of the welfare state in the 1940s, living in London was often a nightmare for the poor; a nightmare alleviated only by visits to the pub – especially those glorious so-called 'gin palaces' with their high ceilings and glittering lights, cut-glass mirrors and a spirit of conviviality.

One of the biggest problems for the poor was the insanitary conditions in which they had to live. Even those in relatively decent housing had to put up with bed bugs, fleas and other insect pests, not to mention rats and mice, as specialist chemicals we take for granted today simply did not exist in Victorian and earlier times. Arsenic was sometimes resorted to if a rodent problem became particularly bad and it could be bought freely at any chemist, but it was so dangerous that instead of killing rats and mice frequently it was accidentally eaten by children who then died a horrible death.

Occasionally Londoners came up with a great idea to improve their living conditions, and having hedgehogs as pets was one of them. These animals were kept by thousands of Londoners, partly as people rather liked them and partly because they were such good pest controllers. They couldn't do much about rats and mice or fleas and bedbugs, but they were wonderful if you had an infestation of one of the worst bugs of all – cockroaches.

Cockroaches were a particular problem in damp areas and as tens of thousands of London houses had permanently damp cellars, hedgehogs were much in demand. The little animals were rarely badly treated because if they were unhappy or sickly they quickly died and back would come the cockroaches. Instead, they were often given the run of yards and gardens which may explain why, until recently, London gardens were one of the best places to find hedgehogs.

The poor hedgehog's recent massive decline has nothing to do with the fact that they are no longer needed as pest controllers, rather the fact that so many Londoners have paved or covered their gardens in AstroTurf or decking.

NAKED KING

The fact that George III was mad for much of his reign was certainly a disaster for the monarchy and a personal tragedy for him, but it had some remarkably positive consequences, not least of which was a transformation in attitudes generally to madness.

Before George was afflicted with insanity, the mad were usually very badly treated. Traditional cures for madness – including starvation, whipping and confinement in the dark – were based on the medieval idea that it was caused by demonic possession. Thus, it logically followed that if the mad were whipped and burned and beaten, the evil spirit within them would become increasingly uncomfortable and leave the poor patient alone.

But when the king of England went mad, people soon realised that a monarch could not be whipped and confined to a damp, dark cellar, even if it was suspected that he might be possessed by devils. Instead, kinder measures were tried (although the king did have to put up with some indignities), and these kinder measures eventually became the basis for the modern treatments of mental illness.

But, as it turns out, George III wasn't, strictly speaking, mad at all. His symptoms were actually the result of porphyria, a rare genetic condition in which a chemical known as porphyrin builds up in the brain because of a lack of certain other chemicals designed to break it down. In some cases – and the king was one of these – the disease leads to periods of anxiety and severe hallucinations.

It was the hallucinations the king experienced that led to some extraordinary antics. At Kew Gardens, for example, he once chased the writer Frances Burney across the lawns with a team of horrified courtiers in hot pursuit, and on many other occasions the king would run naked through his court.

In a moment of supreme folly, which may or may not have been connected to his mental afflictions, George III decided to build a vast Gothic house at Kew. The original estimate for the house was £40,000, a colossal sum in the eighteenth century, but by the time building stopped (with the house still unfinished), the bill had risen to a staggering £500,000. Parliament simply refused to allow the king any more money and the project was abandoned. What was worse was that the house, or as much of it as had already been built, was then demolished.

George III has a curious connection with Australia too. It was his passion for merino sheep, which he had imported from Spain to run about the gardens at Kew (some say he imported them just so he could run after them!), that eventually became the basis for the whole Australian sheep economy. All Australian merinos descend from the small group of animals that once roamed the grounds of Kew.

OLD STONE TO NEW
BUILDING

❧❦❧

As we have seen, various bits of Old London Bridge found a new life when the ancient structure was demolished towards the end of the eighteenth century. One or two of the old stone alcove seats went to Victoria Park and the timber piles made at least one piece of furniture (a fine chair now owned by the Fishmonger's Company), but many people have wondered what happened to the thousands of tons of fine cut stone that was carted away over the several years it took to pull down the old bridge.

The truth is that almost none of the stone was wasted. Much of it was of the finest quality and as it had already been cut and shaped it was eagerly snapped up by various builders of the day. The bulk of it was bought by Edward Harman, who owned the Ingress Estate in what is still officially Kent but is actually now part of London's huge urban sprawl.

In the thirteenth century, the manor of Greenhithe was the site of Britain's only abbey for Dominican sisters. During the Dissolution of the Monasteries the estate was sold and the current abbess put a curse on Henry VIII, which many believe explains why the son and heir he longed for died so young and without children of his own. Some believe the curse is handed down to all those who own the estate, and will remain in place until it is returned to the Dominican sisters.

By the mid-eighteenth century, having passed through the hands of several owners, the estate was bought by Viscount Duncannon and, like all the previous owners, he did not manage to keep it in the family for long.

By 1820, James Harmer, a London alderman, was in possession, having bought the land and begun building the house we see today, the fifth on the site. In the spirit of the times he opted for a deliberately old-fashioned look, designing the house in a way that echoes a vaguely Tudor Gothic style. The new house was called Ingress Abbey – a deliberate nod to the long-vanished Dominican sisters. It overlooked the Thames and was much admired by visitors.

But what makes the house genuinely unusual is that the stone from which the whole house is made was once part of Old London Bridge. Harmer's architect Charles Moreing bought a huge amount of the reclaimed stone, which had lain unused in a stonemason's yard for decades.

So, if you want to see Old London Bridge – as famous in its day as the Rialto or the Charles Bridge in Prague – you can at least get some sense of it by visiting this beautiful house in Greenhithe.

HOPPING SOUTH OF
THE RIVER

❧❀❧

One of London's least known and least visited buildings is the old Hop Exchange in Southwark. Built in 1868, it is the last of its kind, following the destruction of the Coal Exchange in the 1960s and the old Stock Exchange after the Second World War.

Hops had become big business after their introduction to England from Holland in about 1500. Such was the importance of the new plant that it inspired the following rhyme:

'Hops, carp, bays and beer
Came into England, all in a year.'

Ale had previously been the national drink in England. It was made with barley and lacked the bitter taste imparted to modern beers by hops. Ale was drunk by everyone because water was too dangerous – the process of boiling the water for ale made it safer to drink and even children drank large quantities of ale safely because it contained much less alcohol than modern beers.

Despite misgivings about the new flavour provided by hops – one commentator described the hop plant as 'a pernicious and wicked weed' – the new bite it imparted to beer quickly became popular and hop fields, or hop gardens as they were known, were planted increasingly across Kent. The harvest was then shipped by boat and later by train and road to London.

Those who traded in hops needed somewhere to conduct the business of buying and selling so, in 1860, plans were drawn up to build a hop exchange with a naturally lit trading floor. The designer was the little known R. H. Moore, who created the spectacular frontage we see today at 24 Southwark Street.

But the really remarkable bit of the building is hidden inside – the exchange hall is a mass of glorious Gothic windows, wrought iron balustrades and tiled floors lit from a soaring glass roof.

RED BRICK AND SOOT

❦

It is difficult today to comprehend the speed at which London spread during the years 1850–1920. There were few controls on house building and huge profits to be made, which is why speculative builders gradually bought up every available space and London grew exponentially until it measured more than thirty miles across.

Places such as Wembley and Harlesden, Brentford and Twickenham, Leytonstone and Annerley were remote villages in 1850. By 1920 they had all been swallowed up by the Great Wen, as London was sometimes called.

A few parks broke up the seemingly endless rows of red- and yellow-brick terraced houses, and at least the houses were in the main fairly solidly built, but they had a uniformity that only age has softened.

Also, strange stories often circulated about how they were built. Many were put about or exaggerated by builders trying to damage the reputations of their rivals – but many were true enough. Rather than have to break up a terrace to cope with the fact that a spring or small stream had been discovered running across a projected street, the Victorian house builders would often resort to the sort of ruse that simply would not be allowed today. They would, for example, increase the distance between the earth beneath the house and the joists holding up the ground floor floorboards, which is why a number of London houses still have springs and small streams running directly beneath them even today.

Another trick they employed in order to try to introduce a bit of variety cheaply was to change the colour of the mortar used to lay the bricks from which the houses were built.

Instead of the usual, light sandy-coloured mortar, therefore, a darker version would be used. It became hugely popular, but what those who bought these houses did not realise was that the dark, impressive-looking mortar was simply the usual kind, but mixed with soot.

Alternatively, where pink mortar was seen as a useful alternative to entice young house buyers, pigs' blood was used in the mix.

MILKING IT

⁓❦⁓

Milk only began to reach London in large quantities in the 1850s and 1860s, when the railway
network had become sufficiently widespread and reli-
able to supply the vast quantities of milk consumed in
the capital each day.

However, old habits die hard, as the saying goes,
and many people preferred to get their milk locally
long after this was either necessary or hygienic. Until
well into the twentieth century, large numbers of
cattle were still kept in central London and often in
the most astonishing conditions.

The Adelphi, built by the famous three Adam broth-
ers between 1768 and 1772, was just east of Charing
Cross Station. It was a magnificent Neoclassical building (actually a terrace of twenty-four houses grouped
together) that stretched along the river frontage. For
a time after it was built, the Adelphi was immensely
fashionable and only the wealthy could afford to
live there.

But, as the area around Charing Cross declined,
the rich began to move out. By the mid-nineteenth
century, the grand rooms at the Adelphi were being
let to anyone who could be enticed by low rents to
live there.

But even its most unfashionable residents might
have been astonished at what went on in its cellars, for
it was here, deep underground, that a whole herd of

cows was kept. They were permanently housed in the basement of the building and fed entirely on waste from the brewing industry. As a result, they produced a lot of milk, but it was disgustingly blue in colour and had to be mixed with normal milk to make it sellable.

Many other London houses were used to keep cows. The owner of a terraced house in Islington was fined in 1890 for keeping too may cows in his house. Note that the problem was not the presence of cows, but simply that there were too many! The smell and the noise of one or two cows would have been fine, but half a dozen began to annoy the neighbours. The owner of the house kept the cows on the first floor and slept with his family on the second floor. A visitor described seeing three cows happily munching hay in a sitting room with a fine, big, marble fireplace just behind them!

LOST AND FOUND

⁘

One of the greatest and least-known London institutions is the London Transport lost property office. Over the century and more that it has existed, it has been home to some extraordinary items brought here after being found on the Underground and on London buses. Thousands of sets of false teeth, for example, as well as numerous wooden legs, wigs, shotguns, grenades, a set of surgical instruments, a human skeleton in a box, a seventeenth-century landscape painting and even a suit of armour. Other oddities include a full-size jukebox, several record players, trumpets, a cello and even on one occasion a double bass.

A pram was discovered in the 1950s full of empty gin bottles and just after the Second World War a first edition of the 1563 *Actes and Monuments* (popularly known as *Foxe's Book of Martyrs*) – worth around £10,000 today – was discovered on a seat on the District Line.

Among the sadder finds on the Underground there have been, in recent times, numerous children – they are usually unable to speak English and never have papers to explain where they come from.

Dogs and cats are frequently found, along with more unusual pets, including several parrots, snakes, a toucan and even a baby alligator.

But prizes for the strangest things ever to be found

on the Underground should probably go to the following items: breast implants, a wedding dress, a gas mask from the First World War, a stuffed piranha fish, a lollipop lady's lollipop and a five-foot-high teddy bear with an Albanian address label on it.

CANAL MONEY

Over the years, London's canals have gradually been transformed from industrial highways designed to carry coal and steel and other heavy goods to wildlife and leisure corridors. Where once the old coal barges slowly passed gasworks and factories as they crossed London, now those same boats are filled with holidaymakers or Londoners who have decided to live on the canal.

But even in the dark industrial days the water in the canals was never as polluted as, for example, that of the Thames. It may have looked dirty, with odd supermarket trolleys half submerged and pieces of wood and plastic floating here and there, but the water has never been chemically polluted because the lack of current meant there was never much point in pouring effluent in as it wouldn't go anywhere.

It is for that reason that London's canals have always been a haven for ducks and geese and, perhaps most surprising of all, fish. Huge pike up to a metre long certainly inhabit the Grand Union and Regent's Canals and are occasionally caught by anglers who are rarely seen by the general public. London's anglers tend to get up early in summer and are back at home by the time the tourists are ploughing up and down the canal in tour boats.

Among the stranger catches reported by anglers

are crayfish – a sort of miniature freshwater lobster – Japanese spider crabs, and even trout! But perhaps strangest of all was the catch made by a young man fishing the Grand Union Canal behind King's Cross Station in the 1970s.

He had caught several good roach and was thinking about going home when something made him try one more cast. Out went his line. Ten minutes later he reeled in and assumed he had snagged an old boot. Something heavy was attached to his line but it was clearly some rubbish rather than a live fish. The 'rubbish' turned out to be a plastic bag containing £1,500, far more than an average year's wages at the time!

GHOSTLY STICKS

❧⟡❧

A nineteenth-century newspaper recorded a bizarre discovery in the oldest part of the City of London, close to where the first London Bridge was built by the Romans.

This area had for centuries revealed ancient coins and bits of statue, ancient timbers and silver, lead and even gold jewellery. Workmen were said to enjoy repairing buildings here on the riverfront because there was always a real chance of discovering an ancient gold trinket, and in those days such gold would not find its way to a museum. Workmen were never paid well and any discovery of something valuable would be kept quiet and the artefact quickly melted down or otherwise disposed of.

In 1892 the newspaper reported a discovery beneath an old house that didn't involve anything valuable, but was remarkable anyway.

Workmen digging in a basement in that ancient tangle of houses and narrow alleys that once covered acres of ground near the church of St Mary Woolnoth broke through the massive old stones that paved the basement floor and found a set of narrow stone steps descending below ground.

They were able to make their way down only a dozen of them before their way became blocked by accumulated rubbish, but as they cleared this they found a few Tudor coins, a medieval pilgrim's badge and even an ancient leather shoe.

After they had fully cleared the rubbish, the steps were seen to descend much further than had at first been thought, so the workmen brought lights and, in a state of some excitement and no little fear, according at least to the contemporary newspaper report, they made their way down into the 'undiscovered gloom'.

At the bottom of the steps their flickering tapers discovered a small room with an arched stone roof. The ashlar stone had been beautifully cut to create the barrel-shaped roof. The stone walls were of similarly fine work, as were the stones that made up the floor.

On one side of the strange room there was a low, stone bench and in a corner there was a great heap of what the workmen described as 'faggots' – by which they meant bundles of firewood, neatly tied and stacked.

At first the workmen thought the room was merely an old cellar, but it seemed to have been built too far down for that easy explanation to make sense and, in any case, it was too well-built.

The sense that this room might well have been Roman in origin was heightened when the men decided to move the solid-looking piles of firewood.

'At the first touch,' explained the workman to the newspaper, 'the heavy timber crumbled to dust in our fingers.'

Clearly the wood had been in this room for so many centuries that, despite retaining its shape and sense of solidity, it had become almost air.

Sadly it seems that once the newspapers had reported this find it was quickly forgotten, and, in the way of so many Victorian discoveries, that little room was later destroyed by subsequent rebuilding.

REDUCED TO TRADE

O ne of the greatest scandals of the twentieth century concerned the heirs to one of the oldest
aristocratic titles in England. The Sackvilles had lived
at Knole, their huge house in Kent, for centuries and
this house – which still exists largely unaltered –
represented all that was supposed to be most impressive about 'old money'.

Lionel Sackville-West, 2nd Baron Sackville and his
nephew, also Lionel, were famous for doing absolutely
nothing.

Old Lionel apparently had no interest even in the
great house he had inherited and young Lionel seemed
to feel it was beneath his dignity to show any enthusiasm for much beyond a bit of shooting and fishing.

Yet, despite their aristocratic pedigree, the Sackvilles
had a dark secret. Old Lionel had fathered seven
illegitimate children in the mid-nineteenth century
by a Spanish gipsy dancer.

The result of his indiscretions was a hugely expensive lawsuit, which was eventually won by Victoria
Sackville-West, one of those seven illegitimate
children. But, bizarrely, in order to win the lawsuit,
Victoria had to prove in open court that she really was
illegitimate.

This strange situation arose because Victoria had
married a Sackville cousin who had inherited the
title on the grounds that there were no direct heirs.

Victoria's brother, however, was trying to prove that he was legitimate in order to inherit. If he had succeeded, his sister Victoria and her husband would have lost the title and the great house at Knole.

In the event, Victoria won her case and convinced the court she was illegitimate and as a result her brother (also, therefore, illegitimate) lost the case.

It was one of the greatest scandals London had ever seen. Crowds thronged the High Court in London to get a glimpse of a group of aristocrats who, as one commentator observed, were 'no better than they should be'.

Of course, the various members of the Sackville family who were involved in this unseemly row could escape afterwards abroad until the fuss died down or simply retreat to Knole (a house the size of a village).

However, in the bizarre way that Victorian and Edwardian England judged these things, it was considered a far greater scandal when it was discovered that Victoria Sackville-West had set up a shop selling stationery in London. The shop helped rescue the family from financial ruin after the immense costs of the legal case, but the newspapers of the time had a field day pointing out that England had come to a pretty pass when ancient families got involved in trade!

A further scandal filled the newspapers when it was discovered that Victoria had almost certainly had an affair with the wealthy Sir John Murray Scott while her husband was still alive. Murray Scott was so entranced by Victoria Sackville-West that from 1897 until his death in 1912 he spent hundreds of thousands of pounds (tens of millions in today's money) buying things for his mistress.

In fact, it would be fair to say that without Sir John Murray Scott's money, Knole would not have survived with its magnificent collection of furniture, pictures and tapestries. Whenever Victoria had a bill or servants' wages to pay at Knole, Seery, as Sir John was known, was always happy to foot the bill. When he died he left more than £100,000 to Victoria – which resulted in another lawsuit when Seery's family sued the Sackvilles – and lost.

LONDON'S ERUV

O ne of the more unnusual sights in parts of north London, but especially in the Stamford Hill area, is the dress of orthodox Jews, whose clothes are unchanged since the days when large Jewish communities existed in Poland and other parts of Eastern Europe.

These Jews belong to various sects but one of the best known is the Lubavitch, an ultra-orthodox sect that follows the teaching of Rabbi Schneerson. The children of these communities go to schools where they mix only with other ultra-orthodox children and it is said they are taught almost nothing of the ways of the secular world. One Jewish teenager is reported to have looked baffled when Napoleon was mentioned. He had never heard the name.

But life for the ultra-orthodox can be tricky. A man, for example, may not touch a woman to whom he is not related, in case she might be menstruating, which is why in Jewish shops in Stamford Hill you will see orthodox men carefully drop their money into the hands of female shop assistants to avoid even the merest brush of their fingers.

Then there is a vast list of prohibitions, which include not carrying certain items from the domestic domain to the public domain on the Sabbath. Thus, paper handkerchiefs, medicines and house keys cannot be carried outside the home on a Saturday.

For the ultra-orthodox of any faith, Sabbath

prohibitions are a big issue. Perhaps the most awkward prohibition for orthodox Jews is the refusal to allow ultra-orthodox mothers to push their children in buggies on Saturdays.

One solution to the restrictions is the *eruv*. This is a system of stringing wires from telegraph poles to indicate that the area contained within the poles becomes, nominally at least, part of the domestic interior.

Disputes have arisen in the past between the ultra-orthodox and local authorities when Jewish groups have asked that these wires be strung over a wide area in which other groups who are not Jewish also live.

So, if you are in north London on a Saturday and you see a group of ultra-orthodox Jews out pushing their children in buggies, look up and you might see an *eruv*. Technically this means you are in someone else's house or, according to whichever complicated doctrine you follow, in several people's houses at the same time!

HACKED OFF

꧁◆꧂

Compared to the French, the British have always been very prudish. The Victorians famously covered the legs of their tables and no one in polite society would ever even use the word 'legs' if it could possibly be avoided.

A citizen of Lewes in Sussex, an art collector called E. P. Warren, commissioned a version of Rodin's marvellous sculpture The Kiss at the beginning of the twentieth century. The work – now famous the world over – was rejected as too pornographic at the time. The campaign against it was led by the wonderfully named Miss Fowler-Tutt, and no doubt Lewes would love to have it back now!

One of the city's oddest tales concerning sculptures that offended the public taste concerns the figures on what is now Zimbabwe House on the Strand.

Jacob Epstein was a known *avant-garde* artist who had already been commissioned to produce a statue for Lewis's department store in Liverpool. The resulting figure was so well endowed that it was quickly dubbed 'Dickie Lewis', but this doesn't seem to have worried the architect who commissioned Epstein's work for Zimbabwe House (then the British Medical Association Headquarters).

For Epstein it was a huge commission – eighteen large nude figures were to be distributed across the façade of the new building.

The architect seems to have gone ahead with the project without a qualm, even when the striking nudity of the carvings became apparent, but when the building was finally unveiled in 1908 there was uproar. Letters were written to *The Times* complaining that young women would be corrupted by the disgusting display of nakedness. One correspondent insisted that he would sue the architect and the Medical Association under the Obscenity Act.

The complaints gradually died down and the statues were left *in situ* but then in the 1930s the more prominent parts of the statues were quietly hacked off on the grounds that the statues (or their bigger bits) had become unstable and there was a danger that 'anything sticking out' might fall on the heads of passers-by!

Further commissions for the London Electric Tramway building in 1929 caused Epstein even more problems. This bizarre-looking lump of a building near St James's Park included two nude statues known as Night and Day and as usual there were complaints about them being too sexual. Modifications were made, the easily offended went away at last, but public commissions for Epstein finally dried up.

CARMEN APPROVAL

❧❧❧

Many of London's old City livery companies are still well known, despite the fact that most now have little connection with the trade they once governed. The Goldsmiths' Company, the Mercers' Company and the Fishmongers', among others, all run charitable foundations, but they no longer regulate fishing or jewellery-making.

One livery company, however, which is among the most ancient, does at least still carry out an annual rite that has been part of London life since the thirteenth century.

The fellowship of Carmen – or carriers – began in 1277 and their aim was to regulate the trade of keeping the streets of London clean as well as carrying goods here and there. By the early sixteenth century they were known as the Fraternity of St Katharine the Virgin and Martyr of Carters.

They set up places where carts could be hired – these were called caroms – and of course they regulated prices and conditions of hire. All licensed vehicles were to be marked appropriately and by the mid-nineteenth century there were more than 600 licensed carts in London and around ninety caroms.

The arrival of the motor car and the lorry heralded the end of the old company of Carmen and by the 1960s hardly any carts remained in London. The few remaining caroms were demolished – with one exception. It is at this carom – a new place for it is chosen every year – that the Fraternity still marks a few carts each year.

The event is usually held in the summer and dozens of horse-drawn carts and buses as well as motor lorries are brought together and branded – marked on a wooden plate using a hot iron by the keeper of the Guildhall before everyone retires for a celebratory lunch. The ceremony, though having no practical value any longer, is a reminder that carrying goods has always, one way and another, been vital to the prosperity of London.

HORSE WORSHIP

St John's Hyde Park Crescent looks like any other Victorian English church, but it is very unusual in at least one respect: each year it organises an event known as Horseman's Sunday or the Blessing of the Horses.

The event usually occurs in September and the idea is to celebrate horse riding in London, for, despite the growth of London traffic and the loss of green spaces, riding still continues in the capital.

St John's has an especially close connection with horses because it is very close to Rotten Row in Hyde Park, where riding has taken place almost every day for more than four centuries.

Hyde Park Stables still offers visitors the chance to ride a pony along the route that was once used by the royal family (Rotten Row is a corruption of *Route du Roi*, French for King's Row) to ride from St James's Palace to their residence in Kensington. In Victorian and Edwardian times it became a place to see and be seen on Sundays when the great and the good would greet each other here from their carriages or from the backs of their horses. And there was huge (unacknowledged) competition to have the best presented horse and, for the riders, the finest coats, hats, whips and spurs.

On Horseman's Sunday, the vicar of St John's leads a cavalcade of horses to the church to celebrate this equine tradition. Best of all, the tradition states that the vicar must himself be mounted. So far no vicar is recorded as having ever fallen off!

NAME OF THE ROSE

Many ancient London ceremonies may seem rather pointless today, but the English have a great love of tradition – indeed, the stranger the tradition the more they seem to enjoy it!

One of the most delightful ceremonies that still continues in the city is known as the Knollys Rose Ceremony.

The story behind the ceremony begins as long ago as 1381 with Sir Robert Knollys, a resident of Seething Lane, friend of the king and powerful figure generally in city politics. Like all knights in medieval England, Sir Robert was a military man who could be called upon at any time to fight for his king. This duly happened and Sir Robert was called away to the wars with John of Gaunt.

Military wives were used to being left for long periods at this time, which was just as well as Sir Robert was away for more than two years. During that time, cloistered at home and no doubt rather bored, Lady Knollys found herself irritated by large amounts of chaff (corn husks) blown to her house from a threshing yard nearby. So irritated was she by the dust and chaff that she decided to do something about it. She offered a large sum to buy the threshing yard and, having secured it, immediately gave orders to her servants that it should be turned into a garden.

But there was a problem. Lady Knollys' house was separated from the garden by Seething Lane itself and at that time the lane was filled with mud, horse manure and probably the odd dead dog and cat. Without consulting anyone, Lady Knollys employed a carpenter to build a bridge over Seething Lane so that she could reach her new garden without getting her feet muddy or having to weave her away through the *hoi polloi*.

The bridge over the lane irritated the neighbours who saw its construction as an act of arrogance on Lady Knollys' part, since she had not enquired before building if any of her neighbours might object. Eventually the city authorities were drawn into the row and they felt there should be some sort of admonishment of the Knollys. But how was this to be done? Sir Robert was a powerful figure and the city authorities could not risk upsetting him over the matter of the bridge, especially as he was away on the king's wars when it was built. They came up with a cunning solution: Lady Knollys was fined a single rose every year in perpetuity. The rose had to come from the Seething Lane garden and be presented to the Lord Mayor. It was a delicate diplomatic fine that appeased the neighbours and charmed rather than upset the Knollys.

The bridge of course is long gone, but the right to build it in theory remains so long as the rent continues to be paid – and it has been paid every year since the fourteenth century. The single rose is cut from the Seething Lane garden, placed on a cushion from All Hallows by the Tower church and carried in state to the Mansion House where it is presented to the Lord Major. It is known as a quit rent – a sort of land tax.

NOT A BROTHEL

Meard Street in Soho, mostly pedestrianised, narrow and easily overlooked, is one of London's most interesting thoroughfares. It runs east to west from Dean Street to Wardour Street and includes a short run of early-eighteenth-century houses, each with its interior largely intact.

Meard Street was formerly two courts blocked off from each other at the halfway point of the present street and for a number of years it was home to one of London's greatest modern eccentrics, Sebastian Horsley (1962–2010).

An artist and writer, Horsley once had himself crucified to find out what it felt like. He also claimed that he only liked to have sex with prostitutes and, indeed, had himself worked as a prostitute for a number of years. He also insisted that legalising prostitution would spoil all the fun. As Soho became more respectable, he lamented the change and the final straw came when one of his favourite haunts, the Colony Room, finally closed. He said of Soho: 'The air used to be clean and the sex used to be dirty. Now it is the other way around.'

He became famous not just for his lifestyle but also for his paintings of crosses and for his outrageous comments, which were always reported in the newspapers. He was found dead in 2010. The cause was a drug overdose. More than 400 mourners attended his funeral at St James's Church, Piccadilly for, despite his strange lifestyle and drug-taking, he was a charming and friendly man. Nonetheless, many were astonished at the number of people he knew, who were from all walks of life.

Horsley's lasting monument and final marvellous joke can be found at his old house, No. 7 Meard Street.

The sign he put on the door remains and has become part of Soho legend: it reads in large white capital letters: 'This is not a brothel. There are no prostitutes at this address.'

GLADSTONE BAD

⁗⊛⊰⊱⊛⁗

In London's East End, close to Bow Church, there is a statue of William Ewart Gladstone, the great nineteenth-century British Prime Minister. The statue is beautifully made, and the great orator stands, his hand outstretched, upon a fine marble plinth.

Few visitors to London, however, realise that this statue was paid for by the poor – and without their consent. What's more, they deeply resented having to pay for it.

A short distance from the statue there was formerly a match factory owned by the Quakers Francis May and William Bryant. Quakers have a reputation among early industrialists for treating their workers well. This unfortunately was not the case with Bryant and May. Their factory employed girls as young as ten to work fourteen-hour days for a pittance. The rules at work were also rigged to ensure that it was very difficult for the girls to avoid occasional infringements for which they were immediately fined – a way for their employers to make sure the girls' wages were regularly less than they were owed.

In 1882, May and Bryant decided to contribute to funds to build the statue of Gladstone which we see today. However, instead of paying the money themselves, they deducted money from each of the several hundred girls who worked in the match factory. They did this without asking them – an act that was widely viewed, by the girls at least, as theft, and which led indirectly to the famous match girl strike that shut the Bow factory until conditions and pay were improved.

Another statue in London paid for in this underhand way was the Duke of York's monument in the Mall. The Duke, who had no military abilities at all, was made commander of the British Army simply because he was the king's brother and when he died money was deducted from thousands of ordinary soldiers' pay to fund a monument dedicated to a man they all hated.

CAPABILITY GRAPES

Pretty much everyone has heard of the great eighteenth-century garden and landscape designer Lancelot 'Capability' Brown. He worked on the gardens and parks of so many grand houses up and down the country that his name has become a byword for all that is good about eighteenth-century gardening in England.

Few, however, connect the great man with the last of the great Tudor riverside palaces, Hampton Court. Though he is not associated with the gardens here, nor with the house, his connection is with a tiny sapling planted in 1768 in the sheltered gardens on the river side of the great house, but in the protected lee of the walls.

This tiny sapling, which even the most optimistic at the time might perhaps have imagined would last eighty or perhaps 100 years at the very most, grew into a magnificent vine which, incredibly, is still alive today – almost 250 years after it was planted.

The tendency to sweep away the old in favour of the new has somehow bypassed this extraordinary plant. For locals, the vine is as much a draw as the palace.

In the nineteenth century it was given its own house – a special glasshouse that protects it from frost and gives it an early warm boost in spring. A wide piece of ground within the vine house is kept watered and fertilised to feed the huge plant and it is tended by a team of special gardeners who no doubt dread making the least mistake lest almost 250 years of English history should vanish on their watch.

Although the trunk or stem of the vine is now several feet in diameter, the branches that climb from it have been kept to reasonable proportions by the skill of the gardeners, and it is this skill that ensures that every year the vine still produces more than 600 lbs of delicious grapes. The grapes were once given to charity and of course consumed in the house by the royal family, but today anyone and everyone can enjoy them as they are usually on sale in the palace shop in late summer.

MAD WILLIE

If you are in Elm Park, Chelsea and happen across a restaurant called The Henry Root, you might be forgiven for wondering who on earth Henry Root was.

Well, Root was in fact the pseudonym of William Donaldson, one of London's most eccentric writers. The son of a millionaire ship owner, Donaldson went from Winchester College to Cambridge and then joined the navy, but he couldn't wait – as he often put it himself – to get involved in the real life of London. That meant drugs, prostitutes and an extravagant lifestyle that saw him work his way through a vast inherited fortune in just a few years.

Donaldson used the money he received upon the death of his father to push the early careers of poets Ted Hughes and Sylvia Plath, among others. He also funded much of the theatrical boom of the 1960s. Most famously, he produced the hugely successful satire *Beyond the Fringe*, although he was later accused of taking almost all the profits from it while paying the stars of the show, including Alan Bennett and Jonathan Miller, a pittance.

An enormously generous man in other respects, Donaldson eventually ran out of money partly because he insisted on promoting comedies that had no chance of success. Penniless, he became a pimp in a brothel for a number of years – an experience he recounted in his only published novel.

But it was his book *The Henry Root Letters* that made him famous and earned him another fortune, although by this time he was a crack cocaine addict and much of his new-found fortune was to be spent on drugs.

The Henry Root Letters were a marvellous lampoon of the rich and famous. To create the book, Donaldson simply wrote to politicians, publishers, famous sports people, police constables and many other prominent and not-so-prominent people. He wrote absurd but apparently serious letters and then published them together with the replies he received from his targets. The result was a masterpiece of satire.

But drugs and heavy smoking took their toll and Donaldson died, aged seventy, in the small flat where he had lived in Elm Park for more than thirty years.

COACHING INNS

When large areas of London began to be re-developed in the early twentieth century, and especially after the Second World War, the buildings that survived the wreckers tended to be pubs. This is why you will often find a Victorian pub surviving otherwise unscathed in a landscape of 1960s tower blocks.

Two of the most remarkable pub survivors actually take us back beyond the Georgian era to a time when the capital relied heavily on post houses to keep the traffic moving on the many turnpike roads that led out of the city.

The British term 'post office' which came to mean the mail (now used in the USA to mean post) comes from the inns that were once dotted roughly a day's journey by horse apart from each other on the main routes out of London and elsewhere.

These post houses were where a team of horses would be changed – horses had to be changed regularly on a long journey if the distance was to be covered in good time.

Against all the odds, a pub that was once part of this network of post houses survives in the Bayswater Road in west London and elsewhere.

It looks pretty much like any other road in London until you look carefully, as this is actually the old Tyburn Road that ran from the City via Holborn and Marble Arch (then Tyburn) and on to the villages of Shepherd's Bush, Acton, Hanwell and ultimately Oxford and beyond.

The Swan is especially revealing of this area's history. Set back from the road and overlooking Hyde Park, this coaching inn would have been an early stop for the mail coaches from the city. Eighteenth- and early-nineteenth-century engravings show the pub looking remarkably as it does today, but isolated on what was once a road notorious for highwaymen. Hyde Park was then a dangerous place, where every tree might conceal a robber, so coaches would leave the Swan well-armed, and those travelling on horseback would generally travel behind a carriage rather than risk the road alone.

The survival of the Swan, which was probably built in around 1720, is rather wonderful, but some of the tales told about it are entirely wrong. It is claimed that the condemned stopped here for a last drink on the way to the gallows at Tyburn, for example, but this is false. Condemned prisoners were brought to Tyburn from Newgate Prison and a journey from Newgate will reach Tyburn a good half-mile before it reaches the Swan. But stand outside the old pub and look up towards Marble Arch, and with the still unbuilt-on open park on the right it is easier to imagine the old coaching days here than anywhere else in London.

ART AND AFTERWARDS

It is easy to forget that even great artists were once just ordinary mortals trying to make a living in often difficult conditions.

The great J. M. W. Turner rented a terraced house north of Oxford Street, for example, and turned it into a shop to try to sell his paintings – the house, despite its associations, was demolished in the twentieth century.

More remarkable than Turner, however, is the story of the great Italian painter Giovanni Antonio Canal, better known as Canaletto. This name, Canaletto ('little Canal'), was used to distinguish him from his father Bernardo Canal, who was also a painter.

Born in 1697, Canaletto began his working life as a theatrical scene painter. He was also famous for using a camera obscura – a device that showed a reflection in a frame of the scene the artist wished to paint. This convinced Canaletto that distant figures were actually blurred and so he painted them as mere blobs. The effect was to create a new kind of shimmering realism.

What is not well-known about Canaletto, however, is that he lived for some time in a small, run-down house in Soho – and the house still exists. Canaletto moved to London because his ability to earn a living depended on selling his paintings to the wealthy English who flocked to Venice as part of the Grand Tour undertaken almost as a ritual by so many aristocratic young men. When the War of the Austrian Succession began in 1740, fewer English visitors reached Venice and so Canaletto was in trouble.

In an attempt to reach buyers on their home turf, therefore, he came to England, and here he lived at 41 Beak Street, Soho, where he met his clients and showed them his work. He stayed in England for around ten years, travelling continuously and painting the houses and castles of the rich, as well as scenes along the River Thames.

The biggest joke about Canaletto is that his style became so mannered and so copied by others that many critics denounced genuine Canalettos as fakes painted by inferior artists.

SQUARE RULES

⁕

One of the biggest changes in London over the past 200 or so years is the disappearance of private roads and private squares. Until well into the twentieth century, many streets had railings and gates across them to prevent street traders, hawkers and vagrants from gaining access.

A typical street might even employ a watchman in a little house at either end to lock the gates at night and keep watch. The cost to the residents must have been considerable but such was the perceived nuisance of the great unwashed that hundreds of such heavily restricted streets and squares existed.

Almost all have now vanished. Ely Place in Holborn is an exception and here the railings that kept out the undesirables remain.

Some private streets and squares had very odd rules, too, and few were stranger than those applying to Bedford Square in Bloomsbury.

Here the watchmen would make careful enquiries of anyone who wanted to enter the square. The idea was not just to exclude beggars and street musicians and hawkers; it had far more to do with ensuring only gentlemen and ladies were allowed in.

It is hard to imagine today just how easy it once was to tell by a person's dress and demeanour which class he or she belonged to. Great efforts were made by the idle rich to dress as carefully and elaborately as they could, partly to display their finery (and by implication their wealth) and partly to indicate to all and sundry that they belonged to a certain class. The poor and the middle classes had neither the time nor the money to dress in the manner of the rich because in the days before elastic and zips dressing up involved elaborate preparation by a team of servants.

At Bedford Square, only those dressed in a certain manner were admitted. Even the respectable poor had no chance of entering, but there was a problem: tradesmen had to be let into the square or the residents would starve and be without coal and candles.

A solution was reached: the residents and watchmen of the square let it be known that only the owners of the coal merchants, the grocers, butchers and so on would be admitted. This was a problem too, because hard-pressed shop-keepers employed boys and young men to deliver their goods, but not, it seems, in Bedford Square. If they wanted to sell here they had to deliver their parcels in person.

This was seen at the time as an excellent piece of one-upmanship and other streets and squares that tried to ape their betters thought they would copy the Bedford Square rule.

Today the railings and watchmen have gone, but Bedford Square remains one of the finest and least-altered Georgian squares in London. In the 1970s, a concealed entrance was discovered in the cellar of one of the houses and inside was found more than 200 bottles of wine dating back to the 1840s. They were sold for a small fortune at auction and even the earliest was perfectly drinkable.

EDUCATION GONE MAD

Various parts of London have over the centuries developed strong associations with a particular trade or business. Clerkenwell, for example, has always been associated with watch and clock makers – a connection that remains to this day. But one of the more unusual trades associated with a particular area was education. Dozens of schools once existed in that delightful south-eastern suburb Blackheath.

Situated at the top of the wonderfully named Shooter's Hill, Blackheath offered large houses and clean air, which may explain why so many schools were located here in the days when schools were entirely unregulated by the government.

The consequences of this lack of regulation could be unpleasant. Charles Dickens was satirising a typical Blackheath school when he described Salem House where David Copperfield was sent to study under the dreadful Mr Creakle.

Prime Minister Benjamin Disraeli went to school here, as did Elizabeth Anderson, Britain's first female doctor.

These schools began to disappear when, in the mid-nineteenth century, it was discovered that children were going missing from one particularly dubious establishment. In another they were so badly fed that several died. When the headmaster was questioned about this, he explained that they had died because, though well fed, they over-exercised! Even when several children were found to have been secretly buried in the grounds, he refused to admit he was at fault. He said the pupils occasionally killed each other when he wasn't looking and it was the fault of the parents and 'bad blood'.

It was schools such as this that eventually led to laws that regulated education in England and Wales.

STARED OUT BY
THE REGENT

Bedford Square was built in the 1780s as an upper-class enclave. In its early years, it certainly attracted the wealthy and well-born, if not always the aristocracy, and it is a good example of a tendency that occurred across London in earlier centuries.

As London expanded, the rich tended to move out and their once great mansions then usually began a long period of decline. The great houses of Piccadilly, for example, were built to allow an escape from the squalor of the old city, but as tradesmen and shops and other businesses moved here, so the grandees moved out and their old houses were sub-divided and let initially to the less well-off, and then later to the poor and then the very poor. As a result, the buildings deteriorated and were usually demolished.

The rich wanted new houses in areas where the light was good and there was space – and no poor people. Bedford Square represented one stage in this process. When it was first built, there was still open country to the north and so it attracted the city's wealthiest inhabitants, among whom was Lord Eldon.

Eldon had only recently moved into the square when he began to be pestered by the Prince Regent, who wanted him to give one of his friends a job that paid very well but demanded almost no work at all. The friend was Joseph Jekyll and the job a mastership in chancery. This was typical of the time – politicians and members of the royal family often lobbied for non-existent jobs (sinecures) for their favourites.

Eldon disliked the Prince Regent intensely and had been avoiding him because he was hoping to offer the lucrative job he had in mind elsewhere, but the Prince Regent got the better of him.

He turned up one morning at Eldon's house in Bedford Square and was told by the butler that his lordship was ill and could not see anyone, even a prince. Despite his huge bulk (he was enormously fat by this time), the Prince Regent brushed past the servant and lumbered up the stairs before opening the door of every room on the first floor.

He eventually discovered Eldon in one of the bedrooms and sat down opposite him.

Wasting no time, he told Eldon he wanted the job for his friend. Eldon refused and the Prince Regent said, 'In that case, I must tell you that you will never see your wife again.' For a second Eldon must have thought the prince intended to murder him – or, indeed, his wife. However, remaining calm, he replied, 'What on earth do you mean?'

The prince replied: 'Well, I am not moving from this seat until you agree to my terms.' Silence fell and Eldon decided that the prince must be bluffing. He said nothing and stayed in his bed. He got up and went to the lavatory and returned to bed. The prince's eyes followed him everywhere. Several hours later the prince was still there and still staring at Eldon who, by this time, was feeling deeply disturbed. Eldon suddenly gave in and agreed to give the coveted post to the prince's friend.

WARTIME HIDEOUTS

During the Second World War, so many German bombs were dropped on London that a graph recently created to show where they fell left no spaces at all between the bombs; so in a sense it is remarkable that so much did survive.

Thousands of Londoners died during the Blitz and this period of destruction led to thousands being made homeless. But far fewer people died than had been expected.

One of the reasons for the relatively low casualty level was that the London Underground was used as a night-time shelter. And not just the Underground – the Turkish baths under London's exclusive Dorchester Hotel were also used, as was the huge underground banqueting hall at the Savoy. Here, according to legend, a special area was created for 'persistent and serious snorers'!

But the Underground hid more than just civilians. Until the 1980s, it was still a carefully guarded government secret that almost five miles of the Central Line was used during the war to manufacture thousands of tons of armaments.

It was, if you like, a hidden bomb and gun factory. Much of the knowhow and equipment was provided by and maintained by the arms company Plessey. So sophisticated was the operation that complete fighter planes were also made in the tunnels. Meanwhile, the

Piccadilly Line was used to store tens of thousands of art treasures and historic artefacts from the British Museum and various London churches.

IT'S THE PITS

If all the stories are to be believed, there is hardly an acre of London that was not once a plague pit filled to a depth of hundreds of feet with the skeletons of those who died of a disease that, according to some estimates, killed a third of the population of Europe.

The Cumberland Hotel at Marble Arch is a good example, and though this was probably not a plague pit, thousands of skeletons were certainly discovered when the foundations of the hotel were being dug. Most likely these bodies were some of the tens of thousands hanged over the centuries at nearby Tyburn.

But one massive and genuine plague pit certainly does exist in Aldgate, and it gave the planners and engineers involved in building the underground railway a difficult task.

Aldgate (which actually means 'old gate') was at one time the main eastern entrance and exit of the old City of London. So it would have made sense, therefore, to take plague victims just outside the city walls and bury them there. Taking them any further would have been difficult because at the height of the plague the population of London was so devastated that hardly a soul could be found to move the dead anywhere.

So the discovery of thousands of bodies under what was planned to be Aldgate Station on the District

Line should perhaps have come as no surprise. There were far too many to remove them all for proper burial elsewhere and planners in the late nineteenth and early twentieth centuries were not going to let a few bodies get in the way of progress, so the station was simply built in the middle of the plague pit. To this day, if you were to dig through the tunnel walls into the surrounding earth, you would quickly come across the remains of the long-dead.

DRUGS FOR SALE

If we take the historical view, it seems that the con-nection between crime and drugs is a relatively recent phenomenon. By making drugs illegal we made them very appealing to criminals who, of course, exploit addicts to the full in the knowledge that they will be able to get their drugs only from illegal sources and at very high prices.

It is common knowledge, for example, that poets such as Coleridge and De Quincey took vast amounts of laudanum, as did Queen Victoria, and laudanum is simply a liquid form of opium.

But what is less well known is that in London chem-ists until the 1950s, many patent medicines for children and adults, whether for coughs and colds or more seri-ous conditions, contained a pretty hefty shot of cocaine.

The logic behind including cocaine was simple: it made you feel better whatever was wrong with you, and there was no evidence at that time that it was physiologically addictive.

The Oxford Street branch of Boots also sold a medicine known as Daffy's Elixir until well into the 1950s. It was designed to soothe fractious children and contained opium.

Even more extraordinary is the fact that, until the First World War, the most prestigious department store in London – Harrods in Knightsbridge – sold cocaine. Even more bizarre, they sold it in a 100 per cent pure form!

DOCTOR WHO AT
EARL'S COURT

⧉⧉⧉

Fans of *Doctor Who* often come to London and are hugely disappointed that there are no longer any of those distinctive blue police telephone boxes – the boxes that were the model for the original TARDIS.

From around 1910 until the 1960s there were hundreds of these curious-looking phone boxes all over London. But a vast increase in the number of ordinary telephone boxes made the old blue boxes largely redundant and slowly, one by one, they were dismantled and disposed of. The arrival of walkie-talkies and then mobile phones sealed the fate of the last few of these wonderfully evocative call boxes.

But, against all the odds, one such box does remain and it can be found just outside Earl's Court Station in west London.

WILD UNDERGROUND

The London Underground, famously the oldest subterranean railway in the world, is extraordinary for so many reasons that it is hard to know where to begin.

Many people think that it is so solid and ancient that it requires little maintenance. In fact, the opposite is true – when the trains stop running at night an army of repairmen, electricians, track experts, bricklayers and stonemasons descend into the tunnels to check that all is well.

Each day a staggering 50 million litres of water has to be pumped out of the system – the problem is that in London the water table gets higher ever year and will soon have to be kept out of the basements of houses and offices.

In the century and more since the Underground opened, dozens of babies have been born on almost all the lines – the District Line apparently holds the record for the highest number of births. Several murders have been committed on the Underground and on a number of occasions Underground trains have been used in funeral processions.

Most famously, Thomas Barnardo – of Barnardo children's homes fame – was carried to his final resting place on the Tube.

But in recent years the Underground has become

something far more extraordinary – it is now one of the most important sites in London for wildlife.

People forget that much of the system is not underground at all – many of the lines run for miles out beyond the tunnels into the suburbs and it is here that these wildlife corridors as they are known help rare and not so rare species survive and thrive.

Among the animals recorded are sparrowhawks, owls, deer, foxes, voles and even the rare great crested newt.

And though much of the network has been modernised, traces of the earliest days of the underground do remain – Baker Street Station, beloved of *Sherlock Holmes* fans, has been restored to its Victorian splendour by reopening the brick lighting tunnels above the platforms, and at Greenford Station you can still see the last of the wooden escalators.

And while you are travelling about on the Underground, keep a careful eye on the buskers who now perform perfectly legally at many central London stations. It is rumoured that famous singers – including Paul McCartney and Sting – regularly disguise themselves for a day's anonymous busking!

PRIVATE STEPS

If anyone has given the British legal system a bad name – and heaven knows there are many candidates – it is the famous Judge Jeffreys (1645–89). The son of an aristocratic Welsh landowner, Jeffreys studied at Cambridge and then entered one of London's ancient Inns of Court where he trained as a lawyer. He became a High Court Judge and it was not long before he gained notoriety for his utter ruthlessness. Even during his lifetime there was disquiet among the legal profession about his methods, but he usually did the king's bidding and was therefore quickly promoted and eventually raised to the peerage.

It was said that there was only one person in the kingdom of whom Jeffreys was afraid – and that was his wife. They were popularly known as St George and his dragon.

In 1685, after the Monmouth Rebellion (an attempt to overthrow the Catholic James II), Jeffreys presided over the Bloody Assizes when hundreds of those who were associated with Monmouth were executed, often on the most flimsy evidence.

Widely hated, Jeffreys was much loved by the king despite the fact that Jeffreys himself hated Catholics. Indeed, so grateful was James to Jeffreys that he allowed the judge to build a private set of steps from his house into the then private grounds of St James's Park. Until the 1920s the steps still stood halfway along Storey's Gate, close to Parliament Square and right up to the point at which they were demolished there was an ancient tradition to spit on them as you passed!

DOG POLICE OFFICER

Bow Street near Covent Garden gets its name from the fact that the long, curving street was originally shaped like a bow. Laid out in the seventeenth century, the street was later extended north and south, which subsequently changed its shape.

Bow Street is of course best known for the Bow Street Runners, often said to be the first modern organised police force in the world. Less well known is that the Runners' ranks included a dog.

Anyone who passed the old Bow Street Police Station until recently would have noticed two doors: one for the police and prisoners, the other a long-disused iron-gated doorway. It was at this gateway, in 1857, that an old, starved and generally sickly looking dog tried to make a home, only to be driven away again and again by order of the superintendent.

Subsisting on the charity of passers-by and of the men of the F Division, whose headquarters were at Bow Street, the dog soon got hearty and strong and, having always returned to his chosen spot, now resisted all further attempts at removal.

As the various sections of police left the office to relieve the men on duty, the dog always followed them, and as soon as the last man's place was filled up he would return to the doorway. The men, in consequence, became so interested in the dog that, on their encouragement, he took up his quarters inside the station, was named 'Charlie', and was even considered a member of the police force.

Received into the office, where, according to the police regulations, he had no right to be, Charlie, also known as the White Sergeant, was placed on the official dining list and at the Christmas dinner was allowed to sit at the table.

On state occasions, when the greater part of the division was required, a sergeant's armband was buckled around his neck, and very proud he seemed to be of this decoration.

At a Victoria Cross presentation in Hyde Park, more than 500 policemen were present. However, on this day Charlie had accidentally been shut up in a room at the station. As soon as he was set free he went to the park, worked his way through the immense crowd that had collected and took his station in front, at the head of his own division. With the sergeant's armband in place, Charlie sat as stiff and erect as an old soldier in front of the long line of constables. Queen Victoria, in passing, honoured him with a smile.

At a quarter to six every morning, the first shift of men was paraded in the yard at the Bow Street Police Station. Charlie was always present, marching up and down the front of the line with all the importance of a drill-sergeant.

On such occasions he was always accompanied by the only four-footed companion he was known to have – Jeanie, the police-office cat, who, with a bell tinkling at her brass collar, trotted at his side.

Parade over, Charlie headed the men in their march round the area covered by Bow Street Police Station.

At least once each week he set out on a tour of inspection of the district, waiting for a while with any policeman who might be a favourite.

When parade time drew near, however, no inducement would prolong his walk, but off he bounded, always reaching Bow Street in time to drill the men.

When the ten o'clock night relief went out Charlie, after duly doing the rounds, returned to eat with the men who had been relieved from their shift; but as soon as the meal was over he went out on patrol once again, returning to the station in time for the midnight parade of men.

Only two exceptions occurred to his punctuality. Once, Charlie watched for some days by the deathbed of an old constable to whom he was much attached; and on the other occasion he had been severely mauled and nearly poisoned by some of the thieves of Seven Dials, to whom he was well known, and whose schemes he had often assisted in defeating.

But Charlie's greatest feat was yet to come. Early one morning, a constable, while passing through New Church Court, a narrow lane off the Strand, was knocked down by two men. Charlie, who was a short distance behind, ran across the Strand to the police station in Somerset House and, seizing the sergeant on duty there by the greatcoat tail, led him to the constable's assistance. The constable was found to be severely wounded and, without Charlie's intervention, might have been killed outright.

When he grew old and unable to do his rounds, Charlie spent much of his time at the kitchen fire. He died of old age at the police station, in front of that fire in 1869.

DINING WITH THE EARL

❧❀❧

The eccentric Francis Egerton, 8th Earl of Bridgewater (1756–1829), never married. He rarely left his estate and as he grew older became ever more slovenly and bizarre in his habits. He made a servant follow him constantly carrying a large box of snuff; he insisted on wearing a different pair of shoes for every day of the year and he never threw anything away.

As a result of his hoarding, his large London house groaned under the weight of old boxes and trunks, umbrellas, chests filled with old curtains, suits and rugs, discarded wrapping papers, broken-down chairs and tables, innumerable pictures, books, papers and piles of assorted domestic refuse.

But, among all his eccentricities, there was one that distinguished Bridgewater from every other dotty aristocrat in the land: his love for his dogs. He owned over a dozen and he treated them as if they were his children. Some were strays he'd taken a fancy to while walking the streets; others were purebred hounds and gundogs, still others were tiny lapdogs. All were allowed to sleep with the Earl and to eat with him.

Indeed, every evening he would have his huge dining room table laid with the best linen and silver cutlery and each of the dogs would sit in a chair in its allotted place. The dogs were expected to dress for dinner and the only time the Earl shouted was if they jumped down before the meal was finished.

Several times a year the Earl travelled by train from London to his home in the country. Normally one or two dogs would accompany him, but on one extraordinary occasion all fifteen dogs came along. Bridgewater paid for fifteen first-class tickets for the dogs and took over two whole compartments. To make sure no stranger tried to enter either of the two compartments – this was in the days when compartments could not be reserved – he sent his servants on ahead to the station to bar the entrances to the carriages in advance of the Earl and his party of dogs.

During the journey, each dog took a seat in one or other of the compartments and the Earl wandered between the two making sure his favourites were enjoying themselves. Other passengers looking for a vacant seat found the blinds of the compartments drawn and the Earl's No Entry signs posted on the windows.

On one never-to-be-forgotten journey, Bridgewater fell asleep and on waking went to check on the dogs. He found to his horror that six entirely new dogs – 'I'd never met them before,' he declared later – had somehow joined his favourites. Unused to strange dogs, the Earl's normally well-behaved hounds were barking and jumping and biting each other.

It took the Earl and his servants some time to restore order and to reject the interlopers. Bridgewater was so outraged by what he described as a 'serious violation of his dignity' that he threatened the railway company with legal action and it was only a visit from one of the directors that smoothed the troubled waters. Though the railway company officials privately agreed the Earl was a damned nuisance, he was a good customer with powerful friends – so the doggy train journeys continued and, so far as history records, without further mishap.

⟨⟩⟨⟩⟨⟩

No one knows for sure, but Edward II was almost certainly homosexual. And it was his close, almost obsessive friendship with the nobleman Piers Gaveston that led to his abdication and, later, murder. Edward was so besotted by Gaveston that he promoted him above all the most powerful barons in the land and it was a slight they would not forgive or forget.

Edward was born in 1284 and reigned from 1307 until 1327. For centuries after he died he was considered a weak and foolish ruler and then, perhaps inevitably, revisionist historians changed their minds and decided he wasn't so terrible after all.

One very curious fact about Edward is that if his elder brother had lived Edward would not have become king at all and we would have had a King Alphonso instead.

Edward's biggest problem was that he put friendships with young men above affairs of state. His passion for Piers Gaveston and later for the Despenser family led eventually to war with Roger Mortimer, one of the most powerful figures in fourteenth-century England.

Among the extraordinary stories that circulated about Edward, both during his lifetime and afterwards, was that when alone in St James's Palace and elsewhere he liked to dress in his wife's clothes. An ambassador in London saw him dressed in this way and merely commented that the king enjoyed a 'jest that would confuse any courtier in Europe'.

Such eccentric behaviour would not have led to serious problems on its own – effective and decisive monarchs were pretty much allowed to do as they pleased – but when Edward alienated many of his nobles by confiscating their land and then lost the support of his wife, his authority was seriously damaged. His queen, Isabella, left him in 1325 and returned to France. By 1326, she had almost certainly become involved in a relationship with the exiled Mortimer, and with him she returned from France in September 1326 at the head of an army, having decided to depose Edward and place her son (also Edward) on the throne. Edward's nobles quickly turned against him and he fled to Wales where he was captured. He was imprisoned in Berkeley Castle and quietly murdered.

NOTORIOUS

❦

Despite the departure of most of Britain's national newspapers from Fleet Street and its environs, one or two newspapers do still remain close to their old home.

In nearby Bouverie Street the notorious tabloid *The Sun* still has its editorial office. It was also home until its closure in 2011 to the even more notorious *News of the World*.

More interestingly, it was home to *Punch* magazine for decades until the magazine's closure in the 1990s.

One of Britain's bestselling publications in the late nineteenth and early twentieth centuries, *Punch* employed many eccentrics: a sub-editor in the 1920s used to hide pigeons under his hat out in the street and then watch to see the reaction of passers-by when they picked the hat up. He also, when bored in the office, would use his favourite fishing rod to try to hook the hats off passers-by.

Punch began its long decline as television and radio ate into its readership, but the appointment of Malcolm Muggeridge in the 1950s really sealed its fate because for the first time in more than a century Muggeridge removed the picture of Mr Punch that in one form or another had always graced the cover of the magazine. The idea was to try to engage new younger readers. All that happened was that older readers who loved the magazine as it was stopped reading it and younger readers, loyal to *Private Eye* and other modern magazines, refused to be tempted by a Victorian magazine that had simply changed its cover.

The cut and thrust of journalism may have dominated Bouverie Street for more than a century, but something else deeply hidden has dominated the street for far longer. Beneath No. 30 Bouverie Street can be found the complete crypt of the Whitefriars Priory. This stood next to and was linked with the Blackfriars monastery.

The Carmelites started life on Mount Carmel in Israel but, driven out by the Saracens in the thirteenth century, they founded new houses across Europe. Astonishingly, most of the priory buildings here in London survived into the nineteenth century, although by then they were dilapidated and had been converted into smaller houses and tenements. Dickens describes the area as one of the poorest and most criminal in London.

The old crypt was used for storage when the buildings above ground were swept away in the 1850s, before being finally restored in the 1920s and then again in the 1980s.

FREE BOOKS

⋘⋙

O ne of England's most bizarre pieces of legislation is the 1911 Copyright Act, which decrees that a number of British libraries are entitled to receive a copy of every book, magazine and newspaper published in England free of charge.

Although enshrined in the 1911 Act, the right to these copies actually dates back – astonishingly – to 1662.

The idea originally had more to do with censorship than preserving the knowledge and experience of the nation for future generations – which is usually given as the justification for the practice today.

It began when the Stationers' Company – a London guild that had regulated book and other publications since the 1400s – agreed with Sir Thomas Bodley that new books should always be sent to the Bodleian Library in Oxford. At the time, this was the pre-eminent British library – the British Library as we know it now did not yet exist.

The requirement to send books to the Bodleian was enshrined in law in the Statute of Anne, 1710. Today the five legal deposit libraries are the Bodleian in Oxford, Cambridge University Library, the National Library of Scotland, the library of Trinity College, Dublin and the National Library of Wales. But by a quirk in the legislation, only the British Library now receives a copy of every publication by right. The others must be sent new books and magazines, but only if they request them.

The irony of the system is that it was designed to meet the needs of an age when relatively few books were published – in the eighteenth century probably only a few thousand books a year at most were published in England. By the late nineteenth century, mass book production meant the copyright libraries (and of course especially the British Library) were receiving tens of thousands of new books each year.

By the 1990s, that figure had reached hundreds of thousands a year as the libraries felt obliged to keep copies not just of new books but of new editions of books already published. The British Library now has more than fifty miles of shelving and most books have to be stored in huge warehouses outside London. It can take two days for a book ordered by a reader to arrive at his or her desk! A decision was taken recently to try to store more books digitally, but there is resistance to this as in many ways a book, though fragile, is not as fragile as data on a disc.

NAUGHTY ART AT THE BRITISH MUSEUM

❦

The British establishment has always had a strange attitude to the ancient world. For centuries – certainly more than half a millennium – the British education system was entirely dominated by the study of Latin and Greek. Generations of schoolboys ploughed laboriously through ancient texts while books written in English and other modern languages were entirely neglected. For centuries the only English texts studied at Oxford were Chaucer and Shakespeare.

The dominance of classical languages seems odd when one remembers that those most assiduously promoting their study were clergymen – both Oxford and Cambridge existed until recently to train men destined for ordination in the church, yet it seems only rarely to have occurred to them that the texts they spent so long studying were written by people who were pagans – pagans, moreover, who had already been in hell for a very long time.

It was equally obvious to many of course that the authors of the ancient Greek and Latin texts could not have been Christian even if they'd wanted to, because Christianity did not exist at the time in which they lived. This meant that elaborate adjustments had to be made to the design of hell to accommodate those who could not go to heaven because they were pagans, but could hardly been consigned to hell for not believing something they had never heard of.

One of the greatest difficulties with ancient texts and even more with ancient art was that it was often obscene. No matter that ancient sculptures were also seen as the highest achievement of art, something had to be done to protect not just the innocent but pretty much everyone from ancient sensuality.

This meant that youngsters were permitted to study, for example, Catullus, who wrote about men having sex with boys, but risqué statues and pottery decorated with 'obscene' pictures had to be hidden. And this is how the British Museum Secretum, one of London's strangest institutions, came into being.

The Secretum (or 'secret museum') was a closed store where all the beautiful but immoral art was kept. In Victorian times it was packed with statues and pottery as it was felt that young Victorian ladies simply could not be exposed to what today would seem the most innocent examples of nude art.

The thinking behind this prudery was never clear. When pressed, officials would suggest vaguely that women were both easily shocked (being so delicate) and very easily corrupted. Some thought that when women fainted they never recovered; others felt they might instantly become lascivious prostitutes.

Entry to the Secretum was not entirely forbidden even in the most prudish period of the nineteenth century, however. 'Mature gentlemen' could apply for a special ticket, but numbers were limited. In the first years after the Secretum was officially sanctioned in 1865, only two or three thousand people each year managed to get a ticket, but word soon got around and the museum authorities were outraged as the number of applications dramatically increased.

Among the artefacts hidden away for decades was the famous statue of the Tara, a gilt bronze three-quarter-life-size female *bodhisattva* – a Buddhist figure.

Today it is almost impossible to understand what the fuss was all about as the Tara is simply a curvaceous female figure with large breasts. Apparently breasts were a tremendous problem for our Victorian ancestors.

Astonishingly, the vast quantity of racy material in the Secretum was still there, hidden away, as recently as the mid-1960s. It was gradually removed and added to the normal collections in the museum's various rooms and, shockingly, there were no reports of women fainting or suddenly turning to a life of prostitution!

One or two items are still kept in the Secretum today. (If you'd like to see them simply ask to see the contents of cupboards fifty-four and fifty-five!)

Controversy still rages about some museum artefacts – a recent case concerns the Warren Cup. This magnificent silver cup, made around AD5, is decorated with several scenes of men having sex with boys. When the museum bought the cup for the then enormous sum of just under £2 million there was an outcry and, despite the extraordinary quality of the cup, there were many who thought it should be melted down rather than displayed in a museum. It then emerged that the cup had been offered to the British Museum for far less than they eventually had to pay for it, but in the 1960s. It was turned down at that time because, absurdly, the Archbishop of Canterbury was a trustee of the museum.

However, the cup survived and is not at present in the Secretum!

BEST OF BROMLEY

֎֎֎֎

For centuries in England there was a tradition
that wealthy men and women left much of their
money to found groups of houses for the poor. Many
of these houses still exist in many places – beautiful
examples can be found at Abingdon in Oxfordshire
and at Harefield in Middlesex on the edge of what is
now Greater London.

A beautiful group of alms-houses also survives in
Acton on Churchfield Road. These early-eighteenth-
century cottages were funded by a member of the
Goldsmith's Company and though much altered (and
no longer used for the purpose for which they were
built) they are a reminder that London was once rich
in such developments.

The oldest group of such houses in the whole
country, still used for their original purpose, is in fact
hidden away in the London suburb of Bromley.

Bromley and Sheppard's Colleges was founded in
1666 by the Bishop of Rochester, John Warner, for the
express purpose of housing 'twentie poore widowes of
orthodox and loyal clergy'. To this day the college still
houses the widows of clergymen using its charitable
foundation.

BETTER THAN THE
QUEEN'S HOUSE

❦

In 1825, building began on a mansion just a few hundred yards from Buckingham Palace. This mansion – once the most expensive private house in London – was designed for the Duke of York, the second son of George III, and was known while it was being built as York House.

The architect Robert Smirke was first employed on the house but he was quickly sacked in favour of a friend of the Duke of York's mistress, the Duchess of Rutland. She insisted that Benjamin Wyatt be given the job.

Wyatt designed the exterior we see today and this is in fact the last grand mansion in London to be designed in a Neoclassical style. Gothic was already the coming style so it is remarkable that York House was designed in what was widely seen at the time as a rather outdated style.

But the strange history of the house continued when the Duke died long before the house was completed and it was sold unfinished to the second Marquess of Stafford and renamed Stafford House. The interior, for which Smirke was reemployed along with Wyatt and others, was so elaborate and magnificent that it wasn't finished until 1840.

Indeed, this house was so grand that when Queen Victoria came to dinner she stood in the great staircase hall and said to her host, 'I come from my house to your palace.' Whether this was meant as a slightly sarcastic remark or a compliment is difficult to say!

In the early twentieth century, as the aristocracy ran out of money and gradually sold numerous huge London houses, Stafford House was bought by the industrialist and soap-maker Lord Leverhulme. He renamed it Lancaster House after his favourite county and then a year later he gave the house to the nation.

From 1924 until the mid-1940s, the house became the London Museum, but it is now used as government offices. It is open to the public only occasionally.

GRAVE MATTERS

⁓✿⁓

In the eighteenth and earlier centuries London's graveyards were simply places where the dead were buried, but the Victorian love of the Gothic and the macabre changed all that. Wreathed in dense fog and with increasingly elaborate tombs, London graveyards became the centre and well-spring of a huge corpus of ghost stories.

In the mid-nineteenth century all the parish churchyards were closed in central London because they were full to bursting point, and frequent outbreaks of disease were attributed to the terrible state of these burial grounds.

But one such area escaped the general closure and the story surrounding its creation and continued existence is one of London's least-known tales.

The Moravian Burial Ground on the King's Road, Chelsea, was opened as long ago as 1751 on land provided free of charge by the leader of the Moravians in England, the splendidly named Count Nicholas Von Zinzendorf.

The Moravian Church was founded in Moravia in what was then Bohemia in central Europe in 1457. Its founder, Jan Hus, wanted the church to adopt more early Byzantine ideas, including married priests, no indulgences and a rejection of the idea of purgatory.

The Moravians call themselves the Unity of the Brethren, but gained the name Moravians when they left Moravia for Saxony in the early eighteenth century to escape persecution. Eventually they established themselves in London, but they soon needed somewhere to bury their dead.

But how did their little graveyard in Chelsea escape the general prohibition on burials in London? The answer has to do with the Moravians' strange burial practices.

Visitors to their burial ground will immediately notice that all the gravestones are the same size, and are all laid flat on the grass. The idea was to ensure that rich and poor, famous and obscure, were treated identically in death.

But the habit that really let the Moravians off the legal hook was their practice of burying their dead very much deeper in the ground than the Anglican or Catholic Church. For Catholics and Anglicans, a six-foot-deep grave was quite enough and it was perfectly acceptable for further bodies to be piled on top of the first body once a few years had passed.

The Moravians do not allow this multiple burials system and they also bury their dead at least twice as far down in the ground as any other Christian sect. Their graveyard was always a byword for cleanliness and hygiene and that is why it has remained open, in theory, to this day.

BEATING THE BISHOP

❧❧❧

Tottenham Court Road is famous for its shops – especially the 1920s furniture shop Heals – but was once the scene of a most bizarre row between the Bishop of London and George Whitefield, a wealthy Methodist.

A building still stands where Whitefield built his first chapel, but it is not the original. That was destroyed in the Second World War. Whitefield built his chapel here because the land was cheap and he hoped to be buried in its crypt along with the two more famous founders of Methodism, John and Charles Wesley. Indeed, in the eighteenth century, Whitefield was far better known in England than the Wesleys. He was the most famous preacher in the land and in the eighteenth century that counted for a great deal.

However, having built his chapel and laid out its grounds, Whitefield hit a problem when he asked the Bishop of London to consecrate the burial ground. This was an odd request because non-conformists, which is what the Methodists were, disliked the Anglicans – and the feeling was mutual. Inevitably, then, the Bishop refused the request.

Whitefield was so furious that he hatched a plan to consecrate his ground without the bishop's aid. To do this he bought tons of soil from the church of St Christopher le Stocks in the City. The church was being renovated and the soil was available to anyone who wanted it. Having paid his money, Whitefield had the soil shovelled into a long row of massive carts and brought it out slowly to Tottenham Court Road, where it was tipped onto his new burial ground.

As the soil had been consecrated at St Christopher le Stocks, he figured, it was still consecrated now it had been used to form part of Whitefield's new chapel.

In later life, Whitefield went to America where he became equally famous as a preacher – so much so that Whitfield County in Georgia in the USA is named after him.

MOZART IN PIMLICO

❦

The connection between Mozart and London might not be immediately obvious, but legend has it that the young Mozart composed his first symphony in a small house in London. Incredibly, that little house is still there, and is one of a short row of early-eighteenth-century houses built in what is now Pimlico. When the row was built it was a stone's throw from one of the great social and entertainment centres of eighteenth-century London: Ranelagh Gardens.

The gardens are named after Ranelagh House, a mansion that once stood on the site. It had been owned by Lord Ranelagh, treasurer of Wren's great retirement home for ex-servicemen, the Chelsea Hospital.

The late-seventeenth-century house was almost adjacent to the hospital, and its grounds ran down to the river. The gardens are still there but they no longer reach the river – they have been separated from the Thames by the Embankment built at the end of the nineteenth century.

Ranelagh was set up and opened by Thomas Robinson, who owned the Theatre Royal in Drury Lane. He had a keen sense of what the public wanted and knew that a spectacular feature would attract people upriver from London and also away from his great competitor, the famous gardens at Vauxhall, which had been established almost a century earlier.

For the centrepiece of his new attraction, Robinson came up with the idea of what he called the Rotunda.

With a diameter of 120 feet, a central chimney, fireplaces and grand boxes lining tier upon tier of galleries, the rococo rotunda was one of the great attractions of eighteenth-century London.

Much of the entertainment offered in the Rotunda was music, and it was here in 1765 that the nine-year-old Mozart astonished the assembled crowd with his brilliance at the keyboard.

The Rotunda is long gone – the Chelsea Flower Show takes place on much the same ground – but the little house where Mozart stayed before walking across to the gardens to give that dazzling concert is still there in Ebury Street. Remarkably, almost all the other houses in the row have been lived in by the famous – including the great garden designer and writer Vita Sackville-West.

ATTENTION, COLUMNS!

⟞⟨⟩⟞⟨⟩⟞

The National Gallery was built on the site of the Royal Mews – the place where horses and birds were 'mewed up'. It is justly famous though when built the architects were furious that they had to build along a very narrow strip of land – the exact strip formerly occupied by the king's mews.

The gallery also includes the famous pepper pots on the roof – these are fake versions of the ventilation grills that existed on the old stables – and a very curious set of columns at the front.

Most people assume these columns were designed and built for the gallery, which was completed in 1838 to the designs of William Wilkins, also responsible for a number of Cambridge colleges.

Much altered and extended over the years, the gallery remains a Classical masterpiece, and the columns at the front are a key part of this, but they were not built for the gallery at all.

They formerly stood at the front of Carlton House at the bottom of Regent's Street and facing up towards Piccadilly Circus. Carlton House was built at enormous cost for the Prince Regent, but no sooner was it built than he decided it wasn't good enough for him and he had it demolished. The columns from the front of the building were saved and carried along Pall Mall and installed at the front of the new National Gallery.

One other amusing story about the gallery is that at various times there have been plans to charge people for looking at the pictures. When this was tried in the 1980s, it caused a furore and almost resulted in the gallery losing half its pictures. What hadn't been realised was that many of the pictures had been donated to the gallery on the express understanding that the public would always be able to see them free of charge.

This small but vital clause could not be overturned, which is why, uniquely in Europe, the British National Gallery does not charge an entrance fee.

FAILED REVOLUTION

❧❧❧

The Cato Street Conspiracy was a bizarre attempt to overthrow the government by murdering the whole Cabinet, including Prime Minister Lord Liverpool, at a dinner in central London in 1820.

The conspirators, who seem to have been a pretty hopeless bunch, came together as a result of harsh economic conditions following the end of the Napoleonic Wars. London and other major cities were awash with veterans of the conflict who felt they had simply been abandoned by the government. They were jobless and, having fought for their country, resentful. But economic conditions were also harsh for poorer people in work.

Arthur Thistlewood led the conspirators, inspired by the writings of proto-communist Thomas Spence, who argued for the common ownership of land among other things.

What the conspirators didn't know, however, was that from their first meeting one of their number was a police informer and before they could act the attic in Cato Street off the Edgware Road where they met regularly was raided by the police. In the ensuing fracas, one policeman was killed and the thirteen conspirators arrested.

They were quickly convicted and five of the ringleaders have the dubious distinction of being the last people in British legal history to be condemned to be

hanged, drawn and quartered. This gruesome punishment, which was reserved for traitors, involved the
victim being half-strangled on a gallows, cut down
and disembowelled while still alive and then cut into
four pieces.

In the event, the terrible sentence was commuted
and they were hanged and then decapitated after they
were dead. Five others were sentenced to be transported to Australia.

The curious thing about the conspiracy is that,
against all the odds, the attic where they were arrested
still survives in that little street off the Edgware Road.
A blue plaque marks the site.

LOLITA IN LONDON

One of the strangest tales from literary London concerns the publication of Vladimir Nabokov's novel *Lolita* in 1959.

The manuscript came into the hands of the London publishers Weidenfeld & Nicolson, then based in Bloomsbury. The firm had been founded by George Weidenfeld, an Austrian Jew who came to London to escape Nazi persecution, and Nigel Nicolson, the Old Etonian son of the writer Vita Sackville-West and her husband Harold Nicolson.

Weidenfeld and Nicolson feared they would be prosecuted if they published Nabokov's book (it tells the story of a middle-aged man's obsession with a pubescent girl) despite strongly believing in its literary merits. So they hatched a plan to tempt the Lord Chancellor (who was still employed at that time to censor books) into prosecuting them.

Under the Obscene Publications Act, an offence was committed only if a publication deemed to be obscene was sold by a publisher to a member of the public. Without that sale, no offence had been committed. So Nigel Nicolson, who looked after editorial matters at the publisher, sold a single copy to a woman in the office and then told the Lord Chancellor what he had done and invited him to prosecute. In his letter to the Lord Chancellor, Nicolson included a deadline and said that if the firm hadn't been prosecuted by that date, they would assume all was well and publish the book.

On the eve of the deadline, nothing had been heard, so Weidenfeld and Nicolson organised a huge party, taking the whole of the ground floor of the Ritz to entertain friends and family – and, of course, authors. Halfway through the evening, they received a communication from the Lord Chancellor's office which read:

'We have decided it would not be in the public interest in this case to prosecute. Enjoy your party.'

Lolita sold more than 80,000 copies in the following three weeks and established Weidenfeld and Nicolson as a major British publisher.

DEAD TEETH

A Piccadilly dentist placed the following advertisement in *The Times* in around 1790. 'Wanted: human front teeth. Apply to Mr Wogffendale, 21 Dover Street, Piccadilly.'

Dentistry had become something of an obsession in late-eighteenth-century London and doctors and dentists were baffled by the fact that the rich tended to have far worse teeth than their poorer cousins. The simple answer – that sugar rots teeth – was not yet known, but it was a simple fact that sugar consumption increased in exact proportion to an individual's wealth. Thus, in this respect, the poor were luckier than the rich in that they at least kept their teeth longer!

The near-universality of bad teeth explains why in portraits of the time it is almost unheard of to find a sitter being painted smiling. It was not that they did not want to appear happy, it was simply that they did not want to display their appalling teeth to all and sundry.

Benjamin Franklin was an early recipient of the latest in London dentistry – during his residence in the city he famously had a set of wooden false teeth made.

However, by 1800, it was realised that the answer was to replace lost teeth with the teeth of the dead. This may seem rather gruesome to us today, but in the early nineteenth century, when sophisticated materials such as porcelain were not available, using real teeth seemed the obvious answer and a great improvement on wooden teeth. Thus began a huge trade in teeth harvested from the dead.

After the Battle of Waterloo, the trade in human teeth reached its zenith and dozens of poor Londoners set off for what is now Belgium to dig up the hastily buried dead on the battlefield that made the Duke of Wellington famous.

The great thing about these dead soldiers was that most were young and from poor backgrounds, so their teeth were usually in reasonably good condition. As a result, thousands of rich Londoners ended up wearing the teeth of the war dead; and, what's more, there is no evidence that the rich even questioned where their new teeth had come from!

The teeth were cut down and fitted to base plates of ivory which were hinged. Small springs were added so that when the wearer opened his or her mouth the dentures opened too. These crudely made dentures must have been very uncomfortable and they almost certainly fell out now and then, but they were perhaps better than no teeth at all. As late as the 1850s human teeth were still widely available in London and elsewhere.

TUKE'S HUMANE
REVOLUTION

❦

Chiswick House in west London is one of the architectural marvels of eighteenth-century England. The house is perhaps the finest example in the country of the eighteenth century's obsession with Classical architecture.

Designed by Lord Burlington and William Kent, Chiswick House is closely modelled on two buildings by the great Italian Andrea Palladio, whose buildings were in turn modelled on the buildings of the ancient world.

When first built, Chiswick House included a narrow corridor that linked the house to the much older Jacobean Chiswick House. The two existed side by side for almost half a century. When the old house was demolished, the Palladian remainder found itself with a corridor that went nowhere and that corridor still exists.

Then, in the late eighteenth century, two wings were added to the Palladian house. In these the Burlingtons lived and worked. The Palladian core became the house where they showed off to their friends, for here the family housed its magnificent collection of pictures and drawings.

Then something strange happened. The Burlington family fell out of love with their London house and abandoned it; by 1880, the magnificent house was leased to the Tuke family. For nearly forty years, until around 1920, the Tukes ran the house as a lunatic asylum. But this was no ordinary asylum, for the Tukes were the first to treat mental illness in a way that was recognisably modern.

They believed passionately in the virtues of peace and quiet, discussion, good food and wholesome air combined with gentle walks. It was a regime that caused scandal in the ranks of the medical profession, where older hands still believed in confinement and punishment. But the Tukes' results were impressive and many of their patients were able to return to the world fully restored after a stay with them. It is true that they accepted only wealthy patients who came with their own servants – indeed, there were always more servants than patients in the house – but the Tukes' methods changed attitudes to mental illness profoundly, and they did it in this remarkable house in Chiswick.

LEGGING IT

✦◈✦

Over the centuries, many strange objects have been found in the River Thames. Poor children in the nineteenth and earlier centuries once patrolled the mudflats at low tide right across the capital look-ing for anything of value. The prime area was the port of London just below London Bridge because here ships from across the world crowded together and inevitably valuable things were lost overboard that could be retrieved when the tide was out. The 'mud larks', as these children were known, worked barefoot and semi-naked in the mud right though the year, winter and summer, collecting copper nails, lumps of coal and occasionally more valuable items.

Modern mud larks can still be seen with their metal detectors working the gravel banks at low tide and over the years they have found many remark-able and sometimes highly valuable items, including gold crosses, medieval rings, Roman coins and even, on at least one occasion, a Bronze Age shield – the so-called 'Battersea Shield'.

But the prize for the strangest item ever found in the river must go to the contents of a wooden box found in the 1950s, just downstream of Lambeth Bridge.

The carefully sealed wooden crate contained half a dozen beautifully made and hinged artificial legs and two sets of what looked like early Victorian surgical equipment. Both sets were first thought to be general doctor's tools, but in fact they were specialist tools designed to be used by surgeons whose main work involved amputating limbs.

In the nineteenth century, surgeons who removed limbs considered themselves an elite group and they vied with each other to see who could remove a limb in the shortest possible time. Speed was important because before the invention of anaesthetics the patient was given a great deal of alcohol to drink and then simply held down while the surgeon got to work, and a patient in agony could not be held still for long.

The box may have had some connection with St Thomas's Hospital, which is a short distance from Lambeth Bridge on the south side of the river, but this has never been proven to be the case.

ODD MAN OUT

❧⦿☙

L ondon is famously two cities, Westminster and the old city proper. Westminster Abbey is effectively the cathedral church of all London except the City, and St Paul's is the cathedral church of the Square Mile.

Until relatively recently, this dual existence created masses of local rules and regulations that sometimes conflicted with each other, and it is still true to some extent that the City of London is not answerable to the monarch (and by extension her government at Westminster) in the same way as the rest of the country is answerable.

Thus, a free man of the City of London still cannot be hanged using a traditional hempen rope; he must be hanged using a silk rope. A free man can still drive his sheep over London Bridge without having to pay a toll, but if he tries this on Lambeth or Vauxhall Bridge he is liable to be arrested and his sheep confiscated. As well as these, dozens of other strange rules have also survived that apply both in the City and in Greater London.

By an Act of 1888, for example, all cyclists must ring their bells continuously while pedalling; pavements must never be used by anyone carrying a plank; you can be arrested for wearing a red coat if anyone suspects you are trying to impersonate a Chelsea Pensioner; and steam engines and other large vehicles of all kinds must be preceded at all times by a man carrying a red flag (in daylight) or a red lantern (at night).

The rules about red flags and red lanterns continued to apply to buses and lorries whenever London was experiencing a pea souper (dense fog) and until the 1960s it was still a regular sight on a dark foggy morning to see a bus or lorry slowly making its way behind a swinging red lantern. None of these rules has ever actually been removed from the statute book, so beware!

ACKNOWLEDGEMENTS

Thanks to all those who pointed me in the direction of strange stories about London, to the ever-helpful staff of the British Library rare books department, and to Victoria Godden at the Robson Press for making sense of muddles too numerous to mention.